LAYING IT ON THE LINE

Notes of a Team Player

by Howard Griffith

SPORTS PUBLISHING INC.
SportsPublishingInc.com

Director of production, book design: Susan M. McKinney
Dust jacket, photo insert design: Chris Cary
Editor: David Hamburg

ISBN: 1-58261-302-8

SPORTS PUBLISHING INC.

804 N. Neil
Champaign, IL 61820
www.sportspublishinginc.com

Printed in the United States.

For my mother, Ruth Carter Griffith.
Although you left this life 15 years ago,
I still miss you every day.

———————————————

Contents

ACKNOWLEDGMENTS

First and foremost, I must thank Jesus Christ, the center of my life, for his daily blessings.

Thanks to my parents—to my biological mother, though we've never met, thank you for giving me the gift of life. My father, Huie, and my beloved mother, Ruth Griffith, to whom I can't say enough. I'm so glad you chose me.

Special thanks to my wife, Kim, for all of her love, support, and patience. And to our two sons, Howard II and Houston, my proudest accomplishments. You guys are my motivation.

Thanks to my entire family whose love and support is constant. My stepmother, Joy, for being a great listener during my tough times. And my mother-in-law and father-in-law, Richard and Telia Chilton, for always being there when we need you.

Special thanks to my sister-in-law, Karen Chilton, for her assistance in the writing and development of this book. I couldn't have done it without you.

Thanks to my high school coaches, Dr. J. W. Smith and Will Smith—my quest toward manhood started with you.

To Sylvester Crooms for encouraging me to become a fullback in the NFL.

And to all my position coaches: especially Bucky Godbolt, Chick Harris, and Bobby Turner, for not only teaching me the game of football, but also the game of life.

To Mike Pearson—thanks for being the visionary of this project.

Finally, I thank all of you who have contributed to my life, too numerous to name—you know who you are. Thank you for loving me, nurturing me and molding me into the person that I have become. For listening, teaching, criticizing, scolding, laughing, and just for being there. From little league to the "Big" leagues. From Mendel to Julian to the University of Illinois. To all of you who I've met along my NFL journey—from Indianapolis, Buffalo, San Diego, Los Angeles, Charlotte and Denver—players, coaches, media, fans, and friends. I thank you all. It is because of you that I am able to tell this story.

FOREWORD

———————————

by

Terrell Davis

Talented.

Tough.

Confident.

Focused.

Howard Griffith is the ultimate team player.

When I first heard that Howard was joining the Broncos, the only thing I was told was that he was the best in the business. After meeting him, I could see that he had the stature of a blocking fullback, but I'd have to wait and see if he could live up to being "the best." We'd have to go out and play.

It was in a preseason game against San Francisco when I first realized that Howard's tough and confident style of play was unmatched. His willingness to get the job done, and beat the person on the other side of the ball was just incredible. Up until that point, we had played two or three exhibition games, and we were still feeling each other out, trying to find the right rhythm. My job was to pay close attention to his blocking style and adapt to it. I had to know where he was going to block, what hole he would push players out of, where he would take them. Then, in the '49ers game, it all clicked. We found a groove, and suddenly, things starting running like clockwork.

After that game, I remember telling him, "You know what, man? This is the beginning of a beautiful friendship." We had found the perfect chemistry. One that would help lead our team to two Super Bowl championship victories and countless other record-breaking games.

Before Howard, I had only worked alongside one other player whom I liked and respected. So, I didn't expect to make such an easy transition working with another fullback. Very often, change can throw you off your game. Stepping into uncharted territory isn't always the most comfortable of positions. Nonetheless, Howard and I both knew how important our combined performance out on the field would be to the Broncos' offensive scheme.

We had to make it work.

Mutual respect among players is one of the most important components of a team, particularly between a running back and fullback. I can't downplay what Howard does as a fullback and he can't downplay what I do. Communication, on and off field, is also crucial. We had to get to know each other as men, not just football players.

Because Howard was an older player, I realized that he knew more about the game than I did. So I listened. As a result, I've been able to learn and expand my game in ways I never expected. Our working relationship has always been easy and relaxed. I can go to him and say, "Hey Howard, that was a great block, next time take him to the right because I might cut off to the left." Other times, he'll say to me, "Terrell, I'm going to cut this guy in the hole..." So, we always know what the other is thinking. Now, after three seasons together, we do it almost instinctively.

Without a doubt, I know he's got my back. If Howard ever lets someone get the best of me, he takes total responsibility for it. As far as he's concerned, if I don't do well, he didn't do well. His mental approach to the game is serious and completely focused. In practice, during meetings, on game day—Howard's out to get the job done.

As a blocking fullback, Howard rarely has the opportunity to run the ball, but if asked he can stand and deliver. He knows when he's out there, that his primary job is to block for me—a role that doesn't make headlines, but is absolutely necessary to my success in each and every game. It takes a special player, a *team player* to stand in the shadows, confidently knowing that he has done his part to contribute to the team's overall success, whether the world takes notice or not. I might get the glory, but I am always fully aware of who and what contributes to our team's ultimate success. It is because of the hard work and dedication of players who consider great team achievement more important than getting credit for individual performance. That's the mind-set of a team player. That's Howard Griffith.

—Terrell Davis

INTRODUCTION

After playing ball in high school and achieving great success, football was in my blood. In my senior year at Percy L. Julian High School, I knew I wanted to play professionally. The question then became: *How do I make it happen?*

Growing up, you are told that the chances of becoming a professional athlete are slim to none; that so many kids are dreaming the same dream, and only a select few have what it takes to make the dream a reality. This gets pounded in your head early by the folks who love you most, but who don't want to see you hurt or disappointed by getting your hopes up too high. On the flip side, you have coaches and recruiters who think you're the next best thing since sliced bread. So *who do you believe?*

Yourself.

No one knew better than I did what I was capable of achieving. I was fully aware of my talent and committed to making the best of it, regardless of the well-meaning warnings and the blown-out-of-proportion projections. Bottom line: I was determined.

My dominant thought: I will make a way to become one of the chosen few.

Little did I know that upon making this bold decision, major roadblocks lay ahead. No one could have told me, at 18, that the path I had chosen would be one of the most difficult journeys of my life. That's probably a good thing. If I knew *then* what I know *now*, who knows? I might have changed my mind.

Sometimes ignorance *is* bliss.

I knew that hard work and discipline were prerequisites for success, but no one could have prepared me for what was to come.

The first item on my agenda was choosing the right college. When I graduated from high school, I was the hot ticket. Athletically, that is. I had excelled on one of the city's best football teams. I had a name and a reputation for being a skilled athlete with tremendous potential. Recruiters were swarming around me, and that felt good. The only problem was that the school I wanted to attend hadn't given me even the slightest glance—the University of Illinois.

I was interested in Illinois because of its great football tradition. It is a Big Ten school. It had an incredible coaching staff and had made legends out of more than a few players. The NFL watched and respected the team. I mean, Illinois had played in the Rose

Bowl. Mike White was the coach at the time. The team had an aerial attack with the David Williams and Jack Trudeau combination. Top players at Illinois got national publicity. And the school was close to home, just 129 miles south of Chicago.

This was the goal, but getting accepted—academically and athletically—marked the beginning of a series of personal challenges. Though I had been offered football scholarships to other lesser known universities, Illinois offered nothing. Zero. Zip.

I'd have to prove myself as a great ballplayer and serious student in order to make the cut.

Because my mind was on sports throughout my teen years, my high school grades were average at best. Looking back, I wish I had taken my studies more seriously, but the facts were the facts. I was an average student, not because of a lack of intelligence but simply a lack of application. I didn't appreciate the value of a good education until my senior year, but by then it was too late. I had to find a way to work with what I had.

So I was working from a deficit position. And I needed to formulate a game plan that would achieve the desired results. I was determined to make a way.

The University of Illinois is a highly competitive school that attracts high achievers. There were serious doubts that I'd ever be admitted…and even if I was, could I hang?

Could I deal with a rigorous academic curriculum?

It was worth the effort.

I applied under "Proposition 48" and got in. Another barrier tackled.

The academic advisors, however, made it clear that they had cut me some slack, that they had graded on a curve, and had given me a chance to receive a top-notch education at one of the country's leading institutions. I was told that my academic performance would be carefully scrutinized, and there would be little room for error. Fine. I'd take that chance on myself, knowing that the more I was told I could not do, the more determined I'd become to prove everyone wrong.

Now, what about football?

The next challenge was trying to join the squad that had not shown enough interest in me to add me to their roster of freshman recruits. So, without any fanfare—no scholarship, barely getting admitted, no recognition for my high school athletic accomplishments—I tried out for the team and walked on in my second year.

Another block bypassed.

I'll never forget my first day of practice. Coach Mike White said: "OK, we're going to put Illinois back on the charts, and I want you guys to know about our history. I want you to know the tradition of this football program."

He went on to tell us about the great players who had come before us, the groundwork they had laid, and the tremendous accomplishments they had achieved.

The coach's words stayed with me.

In my mind, it all boiled down to one thing: Respect.

If you respect yourself as well as your talent, you can contribute something that is lasting and beneficial. And whatever hurdles you have to jump to reach the top of your trade are well worth the effort. When you meet a block in the road, you must ask yourself: *How badly do I want this? How much am I willing to give?* Here's your chance to reassess, regroup, and recharge. And inspiration comes from the examples of those who came before you, who've primed the ground for your success.

As a member of the Fighting Illini, I recognized one thing: You've got to respect the game.

The game of life, that is.

Whatever path you choose, you must respect the game. Once I made peace with the fact that with choices come challenges, and goals are reached by pure sweat, hard work, and perseverance, I was able to go forward, knowing that success is not an elusive thing, but ALL things are possible.

It's easy to get distracted, even discouraged at times, because the blocks that stand before you appear insurmountable. But I say if you learn to expect the barriers, anticipate the bumps and bruises along the way, through self-discipline and self-determination, you pad yourself, protect yourself and prepare the way for your success. Beating the odds then becomes much more than a cliché, but a personal philosophy that carries you through the toughest situations.

It is also important to recognize that you're never in it alone. Your individual success affects everyone around you. You cannot achieve it alone, nor do you maintain it alone. We're all part of a support system, a team. Whether it is a group that you work closely with in business, a team you play with on the field, or a circle of family and friends who've got your back while you're out there doing your thing—no one stands alone.

Becoming a team player is absolutely crucial to your ultimate success. Learning to play within the framework of a team atmosphere not only strengthens your individual ability, but it also gives you a tremendous feeling of accomplishment knowing that you've been instrumental in moving an entire group of people a little closer to the collective dream.

Through my personal journey as a high school star athlete and a college walk-on to a two-time NFL Super Bowl champion, this book offers solid, firsthand advice on becoming an effective team player. Hopefully, the personal and professional experiences shared in these pages will offer strategies that can be used in any team situation, whether it is a corporate sales force, a little league sports team, a social organization, or a family unit.

For me, football has provided a great foundation for living. It has given me the winning spirit that propels me forward in many areas of my life.

As you will see, I traveled a path that contained many roadblocks, but I learned how to land on my feet. Through it all, the triumphs and the trials, I realized: ***Success has many meanings and winning is within arm's reach.***

1   THE GAME PLAN

"I'M NOT PLAYING FULLBACK. I WANT THE BALL."

That's what I told my high school coach at Mendel Catholic, after he insisted that I change positions on the team, from halfback to fullback.

I thought: *"He's trying to short-circuit my career."*

The coach and I had completely different agendas.

He was beating his head against the wall trying to come up with a better game plan for a losing team. And I was the answer to his problem.

He was frustrated because Mendel's football team was awful.

> *I thought: "He's trying to short-circuit my career."*

I mean, awful. We were beaten routinely, week after week. Nevertheless, I made it my goal to play to the best of my ability every time I walked on the football field. It was a serious matter to me.

All I cared about was playing football.

And I had my own ideas about just what kind of football player I wanted to be.

In my sophomore year at Mendel, as the starting halfback, I decided that I'd create my own running style. I used to run around guys, zipping in and out, which irritated the coach. One day, during a game, he said to me:

"You need to start running north-south."

I remember being annoyed by that statement because I thought I had my game together. A few plays later, he said it again: "Howard, you better start running north-south." I was upset but decided to listen to him. I said: "OK, I'll do it your way; I'll run north-south and see what happens." Minutes later, I ran right down the field and straight into the end zone.

Then, I was mad at him for being right.

I didn't have a tremendous amount of respect for authority at that age. I was a typical teenager.

In my third year, I broke my ankle in a freak

A few plays later, he said it again: "Howard, you better start running north-south."

accident on the field. A player fell on top of me, and my ankle just snapped. So I sat out most of my junior year. My dad was concerned that I'd never play at the same level again. He said, "You've always played with such abandonment, but now… ." He was concerned that I'd become tentative, unwilling to take chances because of my injury. But I wasn't worried. I was already making new plans.

I made a choice that would change everything.

I decided to transfer to another high school, a public school, even though I was going into my senior year. Everybody thought I was crazy—my teammates, my dad, the coaching staff. And nobody believed that I would actually do it. As far as they were concerned, I was putting my career and any potential for a college scholarship in jeopardy.

At the time, I had been receiving letters from colleges all over the country expressing their interest in recruiting me. Everyone was impressed by the attention, but what they didn't know was, those letters were going out to every other top high school ballplayer in the city. Most universities send interest letters to high schools across the country asking high school coaches to name players they believe have potential. Then they put your name on their mailing list, and next thing you know, you are inundated with letter after letter after letter.

I knew what the deal was, so I wasn't distracted by the attention.

I still intended to change high schools.

When the coach at Mendel found out I was leaving, he was furious. So was the athletic director. But my mind was made up.

My decision to transfer schools became final after a single incident made it clear to me that I was definitely in the wrong place.

During a practice one day, the team was running laps, and a sophomore teammate noticed that I was not participating in the exercise, or at least not to his satisfaction. So he went to the coach in a team meeting later that day and told him in front of the whole squad that I wasn't showing enough commitment to the team. The coach listened to him, indulging him in a personal tirade against me that did nothing but break the team down even more. Instead of pulling me aside and having a one-on-one, he listened to an underclassman, a new player on the team, then proceeded to join him in dogging me in front of the entire team.

And I wanted to be part of a winning team.

That was it. I wasn't coming back for another practice. I didn't want to play for a coach who lacked leadership. And I realized it was time for me to cut my losses.

It would be one of the most important decisions of my life.

The athletic director asked, "Why didn't you talk to me?"

What was there to say?

Aside from the personality conflicts the coach and I had, I didn't enjoy the continuous losses we were suffering. I felt I was better than that. As far as I was concerned, I had learned as much as I could at Mendel. It was time to move on, to grow as a player. That's where my head was at 17. I wanted to push myself as far as I could go.

And I wanted to be part of a winning team.

Percy L. Julian High had one of the best football teams in Chicago.

The Julian Jaguars had a winning record. They had won the city championship in 1979, and had made it to the championship game a second time in 1985, the season before I got there. Their head coach, Dr. J. W. Smith, had a great reputation. He turned out talent with the best of them. There was a long list of players from Julian who had gone on to play at the college level, and others who had made it to the pros.

GRIFF NOTE: *Respect your own judgment.*

Julian High School was the beginning of the good times. Things started to roll for me when I joined the squad, playing alongside guys like Corwin Brown, who now plays for the

Detroit Lions; Shaun Boyd; Calvin Seton; and Sean Streeter. With Coach Smith, I realized for the first time that I could play at the next level, that I could have a college football career.

I had made the right move.

Coach Smith has created a lasting football tradition at Julian. His vast knowledge of the game and tremendous coaching style has done so much for Chicago football. He didn't have to allow me to join his team, especially with my coming in as a senior, but when I approached him about leaving Mendel, he listened. He sat down with me and encouraged me to give it some serious thought. He wanted me to fully understand the consequences of my decision.

The lessons I learned from Coach Smith, I still carry with me.

The lessons I learned from Coach Smith, I still carry with me.

I've played for many talented coaches over the years, but no one compares to Coach Smith. In fact, it is impossible to fully describe the impact he's had on all the players who've been fortunate enough to play for him. He's the kind of coach you'd do anything to please. For many of the guys, he was a father and a coach. Parents used to call him and ask for help getting their sons to do things at home. They'd say, "I can't get him to do that…" or "He stayed out too late…" Well, Coach Smith would put an end to the nonsense immediately.

He'd handle it by sitting you down for a talk, where he talked and you listened, or if necessary, by kicking you off the team. He did whatever it took to make you realize that you cannot behave in ways that degrade your family, your school, your community, or yourself.

He was, and still is, all about discipline.

Coach Smith's up-close-and-personal treatment of all of his players stems from deep feelings of

GRIFF NOTE: *Respect the team leader.*

love and compassion. You could talk to him about any problems you were having. Even after you had graduated and gone on to college, you could still call Coach Smith.

He has kept close tabs on his former ballplayers' careers. When players would call him about a problem they were having at the college level, he'd travel to the school and watch practice for a few days. Then he'd evaluate the situation for himself. In fact, he didn't care where he had to go to check on his guys. He often made quick trips to Illinois, Indiana State, Northern Iowa, and Michigan to check on former Julian players.

Everyone who's played for Coach Smith has gotten something from him—whether he's made it to the pros or not, whether he's a Chicago police officer, a school teacher, an entrepreneur, or an attorney. I'm living the life of an NFL pro because of the support of my family, but also because of the one year I played for and became friends with Coach Smith. I owe him a great deal.

SIDELINE

Dr. J. W. Smith, Former Head Football Coach
Percy L. Julian High School

"I didn't want to get the reputation for stealing players. So, I'd tell a kid who'd approach me to go back and talk to his coach. I didn't want them to make a snap judgment. But Howard was different. I told him I didn't think it was a good idea to leave Mendel in his last year. He was captain of the team. He was doing well where he was, and maybe he should finish his career there. He told me, "No, I don't want to." So I told him to go back and talk to his coach and see if things could be worked out. The next day, he came back and said, "I'm not going back there." So right there I saw great resolve in him. Even then, he knew exactly what he wanted to do. That's a little unusual for a 17-year-old."

Many of my close friends didn't fully understand my drive. They'd say, "Howard, it's Friday, so why not go to the movies?" I'd say: "I've got practice. I'm going to the football field or I need to go to the park and practice, because if I don't, I won't make it where I want to go."

I was born with a competitive spirit. And I learned at an early age that you have to live each day to the fullest.

After joining the squad, I immediately began thinking about how I wanted this move to Julian to benefit not only my athletic skills, but also my ability to fine-tune those skills and parlay them into a college scholarship. I had my heart set on attending a Big Ten school. So I worked hard in practice and in games to ensure that I'd have the stats to back up my claim—that I was one of the best high school football players in the city.

I began to seriously set goals—short, long, and medium range.

In the short term, I wanted to win games. My medium-range goal was to attend

GRIFF NOTE: *Set structural goals.*

the University of Illinois, Urbana-Champaign campus. And my long-term goal, of course, was to play in the NFL.

I put my game plan in motion.

Playing ball at Julian was a total experience for me. Under Coach Smith, I was able to strengthen my ability and tap into my athletic skills. Fortunately, I had fully recovered from my ankle injury and had come back in full force, after not playing most of my junior year. Within a matter of a few games, I became one of the featured players on the team. Soon after my arrival, and once the season was in full swing, I was mentioned in the *Chicago Tribune* and *Sun-Times* sports roundups almost every week. My stats were solid, and our team was considered one of the best in the Chicago area.

Our season, however, got off to a slow start. We lost our first couple of games, I believe our first three in a row. The problem had a lot to do with complacency, because Julian had been on top in the preceding season. They were coming off a big city championship, though they lost the Prep Bowl champion-ship. So when I got there, the attitude of the team was set: "We're the best." But we still had to work to stay on top.

GRIFF NOTE: *Allow for transition time.*

I realized that I threw a monkey wrench into some of the players' plans. There was some resentment and friction in the beginning. Because here I was, this guy transferring in my senior year, starting on the team, and getting all of this attention. I'm sure some of the players felt that I had stolen their thunder. There was some grumbling at first, but once we started winning, things changed and everything was business as usual.

Things turned around for us when we played Fenger High School. I believe I had two or three touchdowns in that game, and that's when we started rolling.

SIDELINE

Randall Townsel,
Friend/Former Julian Football Player

"I graduated from Julian a year before Howard. I was playing college ball at Northern Illinois, but I kept up with my high school team. So I'm reading the paper: 'Howard Griffith scores two touchdowns . . . Howard Griffith scores three touchdowns . . . Howard Griffith wins game . . . .' It was Howard Griffith this and Howard Griffith that. So I'm saying, 'How could we have built a dynasty at Julian over the past decade and I not know Howard Griffith?' Well, I found out that Howard had transferred from Mendel. When we had an off-week, my main intention was to go home for the upcoming Julian game. That Saturday, I go straight to Gately Stadium, and obviously, because I was a former player, I was allowed to walk on the field. It was the middle of the game, and there was Howard in uniform, standing on the sideline. So, I walked up to him, tapped him on the shoulder, and said, "Hey, I'm Randall Townsel. Are you Howard Griffith?" He answered, "Yeah, I'm Howard." We laughed, talked, exchanged information and became friends from that day forward."

After each game, there would be stories about my performance: "Griffith ran five times for 102 yards in the first quarter"; "Howard Griffith returned a 52-yard punt to tie the score." It was an incredible time for me. I worked extremely hard in practice. On game day, it all paid off.

Replay

MY SENIOR YEAR, *I played in what I now consider one of the best games of my career. It was a five-overtime thriller against Simeon High School. It was pouring down rain. There was probably a quarter inch of water on the field. Every time you took a step, water splashed in every direction.*

Once we went into overtime, I got the ball and scored. The crowd went crazy. And so did I. I was so excited that I took the ball and heaved it to the other end of the field. Big mistake. Our team received a five-yard penalty, which meant Simeon lined up on the five. They scored. So Coach Smith looks at me and says, "You owe me." The game heated up in each OT. We were all out there scrambling, trying to make a play that would give us the win. The clock just kept ticking—another OT, then another, and yet another. And in the end, I ran the screen for a touchdown in the fifth overtime! We won the game. To this day, I'm not big on huge shows of emotion in the end zone. But, hey, all's well that end's well … right?

Taylor Bell, a long-time prep sports writer, wrote that that game was one of the best games he had ever seen.

When I was out on the field, I was on top of the world. There was no better feeling.

Football helped get me through some tough times.

THE FIRST ORGANIZED SPORT I ever played was hockey. I loved to go ice skating at the University of Chicago campus in Hyde Park. There was always a good hockey game going on there. One day some fellas came over to me asking, "Howard, do you want to play on our team?" I accepted, but only as an experiment—an experiment that didn't last but a day. I knew hockey wasn't my sport, but I loved competing.

I started playing baseball when I was about nine years old. I skipped the Pee Wee league and played in the Pony League for four years. That was during the time when baseball was big in Chicago, around 1977. The coaches could see that I had natural athletic ability, even though I was just a little kid. My parents were excited. My dad loves baseball, so he encouraged me to play the game. And I'm sure my mother thought of baseball as a safe sport, where I wouldn't get too banged up. So, by the time I was 13, I was a serious little baseball player, playing left field, catcher, and sometimes shortstop in parks all over the city.

> *I knew hockey wasn't my sport, but I loved competing.*

I realize now that participating in organized team sports contributed a great deal to my self-esteem and early development. Most of the baseball coaches I played under had a community consciousness, meaning they understood the values that we were taught at home. So they made sure that those principles of pride and decency were enforced during away games, when our parents weren't present.

The coaches were usually from the South Side, with kids of their own playing on the team. There was a real family atmosphere, which is so important. My parents never worried about me when I traveled with the team. They knew all of the coaches well, and they trusted them.

My parents, both educators, were born and raised in Arkansas. There is actually a town called Griffith Town, named after my dad's father, who had contributed a great deal to the development of the town. Everybody knew him. My dad, Huie, is from a family of nine brothers and sisters. So the Griffiths were everywhere. And my mother's family was from a neighboring town, Sparkman, Arkansas.

In the Bible, the name Ruth means "the compassionate one," and that describes my mother, Ruth Carter Griffith, perfectly. She was incredible. When I think back to my childhood days, I have vivid memories of my mom and dad entertaining company, having card parties and big family dinners. My mother was the glamorous type. She was always dressed to the nines and loved the best of everything.

In 1980, when I was 12 years old, my mom was diagnosed with breast cancer. She had a mastectomy and went into remission for a while, but it didn't take long for the cancer to come back. For five years, she battled the disease. During this time, I was an adolescent, and needless to say, her illness only added fuel to my fire. I was always into something.

My problem was my temper. I was rebellious and disobedient. At one point, my parents tried to get me counseling.

I had an angry undercurrent that no one understood. I didn't even know where all of the bottled-up anger was coming from. So, I'd end up in fights and arguments, which just drove my mother crazy.

I grew up in a quiet, middle-class South Side community, but Chicago's one of those cities where three blocks in one direction, or across the tracks in the other, puts you in an entirely different kind of space. And there were several big high schools in the area, which meant lots of teenagers.

The local hangout was the neighborhood burger joint, Wendy's, and everything went down in there. I certainly spent a good amount of my time hanging out and had my share of...*altercations.* I was such a wild child at that time, that if anybody said the wrong thing to me, we were going to fight.

GRIFF NOTE: *Lack of self-control distracts you from your goal.*

I had a real problem with self-control. My friends used to call me "short fuse."

In retrospect, of course, I regret causing so many problems for my parents, especially my mother, who worried about me constantly and was seriously ill during those years.

In fact, at the same time that I was hanging out and acting like a crazy teenager, I was also responsible for driving my mother to her weekly chemotherapy sessions.

As the weeks and months progressed, she began to lose her battle with cancer.

I watched her die gradually.

I'll never forget the final days. She was hooked up to so many machines. There was one that charted heartbeats, and an-

"Don't cry, honey. Be strong."

other one that monitored oxygen levels. And she knew it was over. One day in particular, I remember, I was sitting by her side and she just started to cry. When I returned the following day, I looked at the monitors and I could see the indicators dropping. I don't remember the exact numbers. I only remember them dropping: 70/69; then it would read 69/65. I could literally see her passing away. As the numbers decreased, I cried and cried. I remember her looking at me, holding my hand, and saying, "Don't cry, honey. Be strong."

Eventually, it became too much, so I left.

My dad received an emergency call later that evening to come to the hospital. I chose not to go.

Instead, I caught up with my buddy, Carrie Williams, and for some reason, we went to see a woman who'd been like a second mother to me. That's when I received the most shocking news of my life. She said, "Howard you should feel lucky that they chose you."

"*Chose* me?"

"For adoption."

"*Adoption?*"

She had no idea that I didn't know. I was overloaded, dazed, and completely confused. After that, I remember Carrie and I went to the store and bought some beer. I was real hot because I hadn't been told. My mother was dying, or the woman I had believed all my life was my mother. I don't even have the words to describe how it felt.

Eventually, I went home and got in bed. But I couldn't sleep. I finally drifted off and discovered later that it was the exact time of my mother's death. My father came home late at night and told me she had passed away. But I don't remember any of it. I had fallen into a deep, deep sleep.

When I woke up, denial took over. I started working around the yard. We always wanted the best-looking lawn on the block, so the first thing I did was grab the lawn mower.

"Did you hear what I said last night?" my dad asked. "Did you hear what I said?"

But I shut it off. I kept doing the things I would normally do. It could've been any ordinary Saturday. Obviously, the phone was ringing off the hook, and people were streaming in. The house was packed. My mother had been involved in a sorority, church groups, and other social organizations, so she was fairly well known in the community.

I didn't want to be there, so I went to see my friend Roscoe and his mom. She took me to a department store so I could buy a suit for the funeral. I didn't go to the funeral home or involve myself in the handling of arrangements. I don't even remember most of the details of the days that followed, but I do remember picking out a suit that was identical to the colors of the casket—gray with burgundy trim.

SIDELINE

Dr. J. W. Smith, Former Head Football Coach
Percy L. Julian High School

"His mother's death was a defining moment in his life. I think he reached down into himself, as he's been able to do throughout his life, and pull himself together from within. Prior to games, big games, any games, he changes. He gets in a different mode, and you leave him alone. A look comes over him. He begins to look inward."

Before the wake, everyone gathered at our house. I distanced myself from the whole thing. So when everyone left to go over to the church, I stayed behind. I wanted to go through the experience on my own terms.

I finally made it to the wake, an hour or so after everyone else.

I remember when I walked in, everyone crowded around me, trying to console me, telling me that everything was going to be all right. Oddly enough, at that point, I was calm and composed. In fact, I was fine. Most of those who had come to reassure *me* were having a harder time keeping *their* composure.

Thinking back, I went into automatic pilot and took over the whole thing. Everyone was coming up to me, saying things like

"Howard, whatever you need. Everything is going to be fine." And I'd say, "Hey, don't worry about me." Then my mom's best friends, Pearlie and Audrey Williams and Mrs. Higgenbotham, came by and we kind of huddled around each other. I put my arms around them and said: "Well, we have to do a good job. We have to take care of everything that needs taking care of, and you guys have to watch out for me now."

To this day, they are stunned by how well I held it together. They had

I promised her I would be the best football player I could be.

known me all my life. And no one could believe it the next day, when I gave the eulogy at the funeral.

People were scared I'd fall apart emotionally. But I didn't. In fact, everyone said I was eloquent. They couldn't believe what came out of my mouth. I hadn't prepared. I just said what I felt.

That evening, I told my mom I wanted to be the best person I could be. I promised her that I would become the best football player I could be. I talked about our relationship and how I'd made it so difficult for her. And that I loved her.

I didn't break down until they closed the casket. Then, I lost it. I couldn't handle it at that point.

My mother had been preparing me for her death the entire time she was ill. When I used to visit her in the hospital, she would always talk to me about getting prepared for what was going to happen.

She died when I was a junior in high school. The year before I joined the Julian team.

She meant everything to me. And her passing affected me deeply.

The day of the funeral, I realized how much I owed my parents. They gave me a powerful sense of will. They taught me that you can not allow outside distractions to keep you from achieving your goals.

Football became my outlet.

The game consumed me.

Back then, my friends and I used to watch Walter Payton and the Chicago Bears on Sundays; then, when their game was over, our game would begin. All into the night, we were in the park playing tackle football.

I never forgot the promise I made to my mother. I had a game plan. It was simple: To listen, learn and execute to the best of my ability.

I was willing to lay it all on the line in order to keep my promise.

GRIFF NOTES

When you are part of a team, some of the most important work that you do is individual work. Before you can become a beneficial, contributing player on the team, you must determine what your own strengths and weaknesses are, what your personal goals are, and what your contribution will be to the whole.

- **Respect your own judgment.**

Every team has a leader, yes; but as a team player, you represent secondary leadership. Your input is valuable and necessary to the team's overall function. In order for your teammates to trust *you,* you must trust and respect your own judgment. Don't be afraid to step out on faith, and always be ready to back up your plan, suggestion, or point of view.

- **Respect the team leader.**

The team leader is at the helm. Before joining a team—whether it's a corporate sales force, a Little League team, or a social organization—take a look at how things are run from the top. If, from your perspective, the leader appears capable, with the ability to move the team from point A to point B, you will likely respect and work well under his or her leadership.

On the other hand, if you take issue with how the team or organization is run, that may not be the team for you. It takes a symbiotic relationship between a team leader and his or her players in order to create a great team dynamic, where there is mutual respect and cooperation.

• **Allow for transition time on a team.**

Patience is the key. When you are the new player on the team, allow time for the other players to adjust to your presence. It may take awhile. But your focus should be on the business at hand—winning the game, the campaign, the bid, or the sales goal. Whatever the team's goal, concentrate on contributing your part.

• **Set structural goals.**

Short-term, medium-range, and long-term goals. You've heard it all before. Goal planning is important. It serves to keep you focused and on track. As a team player, it is your job to move the team closer to the team goal. In addition, you should set individual goals that work within the framework of the team's overall scheme. Your own personal goals will keep you motivated and inspired throughout the journey. They will remind you of why you've joined the team in the first place.

- **Lack of self-discipline distracts from the goal.**

Self-discipline is an inside job. It takes a conscientious player to address his or her problem areas and find effective resolutions. It is unfair to expect your teammates to resolve your personal issues, particularly those that stem from lack of self-discipline or self-control. They are big negatives in a team atmosphere. It is up to each player on a team to check his or her ego, control issues, and pride issues, at the door. A team is a unit. Selfishness, self-destructive behavior, and undisciplined behavior only serve to bring the whole team down.

Creating a Game Plan

Determine exactly what you'd like to achieve, in specific detail. In a team situation, everyone should be working from the same set game plan. Every aspect of the plan must incorporate each player's talents and input. And though each person may have a different job, the end result should be the complete execution of the game plan that brings about the accomplishment of the team's set goals.

Understand the opposition. Pay close attention to the competition. Taking a closer look at the ways in which they could possibly beat you at your own game helps you to better prepare and tighten your own game plan to make it as foolproof as possible. Anticipate the actions the opposition may take to keep you from achieving success.

Prepare for the unexpected. Your game plan must be flexible enough to allow for adjustments along the way. If you find that a certain aspect of your plan isn't working, make the adjustment immediately. If you are distracted by unexpected or unforeseen incidents in your personal life, find ways to handle them outside of the team atmosphere. Another option, of course, would be to channel that energy into your work. Allow your work to be the outlet for any personal frustration or difficulties you're experiencing.

Opposition comes in many forms. At times, you can be your own worst enemy. Always keep yourself in check and ask yourself if you're doing all you can to contribute to the execution of the game plan. Teams are usually weakened from the inside out, from behaviors that are destructive and unhealthy (e.g., procrastination, lack of communication, lack of focus.) Make sure that you're not guilty of being the weak link.

Aspects of a Solid Game Plan

In football, when we lay down our game plan, one of the most critical parts of that plan is **learning your opponent.** That's where we start. We take a long, hard look at our opponent by studying its past performance, their style of play, their strengths and weaknesses, assets and deficits, its overall record. We watch hours and hours of tape, and in so doing, we **learn the opponent** and can therefore anticipate the strategies that the opponent will put into play in order to stop us from achieving success. In many ways, this kind of preparation allows you to recognize roadblocks before you get to them.

2   TEAM ROSTER

AT THIS POINT, THE LOCAL MEDIA BEGAN TO FOLLOW my football career closely, and there was real interest from scouts and recruiters. However, it was a time of great transition for me. While I was making great strides in high school sports, I was still trying to resolve some personal issues at home. I was silently grieving the loss of my mother. And my dad and I were having serious trouble getting along. We were bumping heads. Then, there was the added complication of my grades, which were slipping.

The adoption news was a shock to my system, to say the least, but over time, I came to terms with it. However, part of the problem was that my dad and I never discussed it. Although I confronted

"Why didn't they tell me?"

him immediately, there was no sit-down talk or explanation. I still had questions, most important:

Why didn't they tell me?

I have one particularly strange childhood memory.

We used to go down to Arkansas to visit my mother's family every summer. One day, while sitting on the porch, I said:

"I want to go back with Mary. I want to go back where I was before."

I was referring to the people at the orphanage. I was very young, but I made this comment, from time to time, throughout my early childhood. Then I'd see the shocked look on their faces. Their reaction said, "How in the world does he remember?"

I was three years old when my parents adopted me.

I'm sure they had questions and concerns about my family background. The very nature of adoption breeds uncertainty. There are so many things you just don't know, and may never know. They didn't know my background. So they probably had some lingering questions about me that could only be answered as my life unfolded, as I grew older.

SIDELINE

Huie Griffith,
Howard's father

"When we decided to adopt a child, the process took years. I was picky, but Ruth was pickier than me. Even the lady from the agency said, 'I don't know if there's anybody good enough for you Griffiths.' Well, they took us to this little boy who was playing by himself with a little push truck. As soon as Ruth saw him, she shouted, 'That's my baby! He's the one!' If you've seen the disarming smile Howard has now, well, he threw it on her that day when he was three years old."

I've often wondered about my natural parents: Do they know who I am? Have they seen me in the newspaper or on television? Is my face familiar?

As recently as last year, I tried locating them. The orphanage I was placed in has since closed, so I haven't had much luck. But they've had plenty of chances to come forward because I've had so much press as an athlete, especially in Chicago.

My father eventually remarried. Before his new wife, Joy, moved in with us, one of the first things she said was: "Listen, Howard. I'm not coming in trying to replace your mother or anything like that." From that day forward, we've never had a problem with one another. Actually, Joy was a buffer between my father and me during the period when we were working through our differences, dealing with the death of my mom, and the whole adoption thing. Things were tense for a while. I had met my future wife,

Kim, around that time as well, and we started dating, which helped divert my attention from the problems at home.

Eventually, my dad and I were able to get back to the good relationship we'd always had.

My dad and I are both realists. So we dealt with it. We faced it. And we went on. We never sat down and talked about it in detail until much later, maybe even two years later.

But the other hot issue at the time was my college choice.

College scouts made their regular rounds at Julian, so I received offers from universities in the Midwest. Southern Illinois, Northern Iowa, Illinois State University, and Holts Junior college made generous offers. As a matter of fact, Southern Illinois made concessions on behalf of four or five other players I knew, after I told SIU's recruiters that I wasn't interested in attending their school because none of my friends were going there. They let those guys in with the hopes that I'd reconsider their offer.

SIDELINE

Kim Griffith, Howard's wife

"Around this time, Howard and I met and started dating. I remember there being a whole lot of discussion about his college choice, scholarship offers, and his football career. It was an intense time for him. I stayed out of the discussions, for the most part. I had decided to attend Purdue University in Indiana, and I hoped that he would attend a school nearby. I also knew that his heart was set on Illinois, but Southern was making such generous offers that some people around him thought he should take full advantage of that opportunity. To some, it didn't make sense that he had such high hopes to attend a school that hadn't given him any attention. But if you know Howard, you knew that one way or the other, he'd find a way to get what he was after."

There was a mixture of advice floating around—that maybe I should go to

GRIFF NOTE: *Respect your better judgment.*

junior college since my grades weren't up to par, give myself more time to refine my football skills, that I could be a big fish in a small pond at a smaller school.

But I sat down with Coach Smith and discussed the pros and cons of each offer. He didn't want to be the one to make the final decision—*that was my job.* But he did show me how to weed through all of the information, how to decipher it and understand exactly what each school was offering. After a thorough discussion, I told him point-blank that I didn't want to go to junior college, nor did I want to attend any of the universities that were offering full four-year scholarships.

I wanted to attend the University of Illinois.

I knew full well that my

GRIFF NOTE: *Stick to your game plan.*

grades weren't good enough for Illinois, but we had to find a way. Coach Smith decided he would speak directly with Mike White, the head coach of the Illinois football team.

SIDELINE

Dr. J. W. Smith, Former Head Football Coach
Percy L. Julian High School

"Howard could see down the line. I could see down the line with him. It was obvious he was going to be a tremendous football player. We sat down and had a long talk one day. He said, 'I know I'm better than that. I don't want to go to any these schools. I want to go to Illinois.' We talked about all of the circumstances. It's always good to have a good reputation. So Mike and I talked. Mike said, 'I'll take him. We'll put him on Prop 48 status.' That first year, he worked like I-don't-know-what on the books, in the weight room, in every area, to prepare himself.

"One thing I never understood: Why do so many people underestimate Howard? I've seen the look in his eyes when somebody tells him he doesn't have the ability to reach such-and-such goal. How could anyone think that? Can't they see his fire? Mike White knew what was going on. He could see something in Howard's eyes."

When I joined the Illinois squad in 1986, I was a Proposition 48 walk-on, which meant my freshman year of college was not under scholarship. And I was redshirted, which meant I wasn't allowed to play ball until I got my grades up.

The pressure was on.

Everyone had big expectations, especially my father, who wanted me to buckle down and become a good student. It was my idea to apply to Illinois and turn down full four-year scholarships.

Needless to say, I was expected to deliver.

The pressure was on.

GRIFF NOTE: *Respect the team legacy.*

The first thing I learned at the college level: You're wearing the university on your chest.

The feats I had accomplished in high school no longer mattered. I was not a solo act. There would be no local press shouting my glory. I'd have to work hard and essentially, prove myself all over again.

My ultimate goal was to play in the big league—the NFL. I believed Illinois could get me there.

SIDELINE

Randall Townsel,
Friend/Former Julian Football Player

"When I found out that Howard was planning to attend Illinois, I thought that was the right move for him. Most of the guys coming out the Julian program possessed what it took to go further, whether at the college level or the pros. Howard had the talent, and Illinois would give him exposure. At Illinois they'd be playing against Big Ten schools—

Ohio State, Michigan. And he'd be playing with other great athletes like Henry Jones and Mike Bellamy. Those are the kind of games and players that attract the attention of scouts."

They say experience is the best teacher, and if that's true, I've been taught well. I already knew what results I'd get by not taking my studies seriously, so I made a 360-degree turnaround. I became a speech/communications major, carrying the maximum number of hours per semester with little time left for messing around. But I had a great incentive: football.

GRIFF NOTE: *Make necessary adjustments.*

I knew if I did well, no one could keep me from it. I wanted to succeed at Illinois, so I created the circumstances to get things moving in a positive direction.

My weekly routine was de-

GRIFF NOTE: *Set a disciplined work ethic.*

manding. I was working hard, studying and training, but I wasn't allowed to practice at the time. I did things the right way in the short term so that my long-term goals could be actualized. I stuck to my game plan.

My freshman year, I dedicated all my time to my classes to get my grades up.

SIDELINE

Quintin Parker,
Former Illinois Strong Safety

"I think playing college ball is as intense as being a professional of any sort, just because the expectations of you as a young person are so high. You're expected to perform under intense pressure, in front of millions of people. You're asked to do things that you've never been asked to do before. When we first got to Illinois, we had meetings around seven in the morning, before we even went to class. Then we'd go to class, lunch would be about 25 minutes, and then we had practice. Because of the high expectations, you had to get to everything early. You wanted the coaches to see you in there looking at film, preparing for the upcoming game. You didn't get any down time until maybe 11:00 or 12:00 at night. But by then, it was time to study."

SIDELINE

David Paoni
Friend/Illinois graduate

"Howard was not the typical football player; he was more a student than football player. He had an incredible way of balancing his friendships with the team and staying out of trouble. It was not hard to get into trouble, and he always managed to make the right decisions. Howard was well liked, and it was impossible to walk around campus with him because he was being stopped left and right by people whom he befriended. Most football players were not well liked because of the swagger they walked around with, but not Howard. He was popular with all different kinds of people. That characteristic is what separates Howard from other athletes. He can make anyone around him feel good about themselves."

In my second year, I played on special teams. I was also a scout-team player who serviced our de-

GRIFF NOTE: *Utilize every opportunity.*

fense, running offensive plays. In fact, quarterback Jeff George and I were on the scout team together. This wasn't exactly where I wanted to be, but I knew if I was out there, getting the attention of the coaching staff, at some point they'd have to take notice. It was an extremely humbling experience.

There were coaches, like the defensive coach, who thought I was good enough to be playing, but others never forgot the fact that I was a walk-on, which has a certain stigma attached. Prop 48 status never bothered me much, for several reasons. First, I never considered myself to be ineducable, so I didn't allow teachers or coaches to treat me as some special case. Second, Prop 48 took football away from me that first year, which made me realize just how important playing was to me. And finally, Prop 48 got me into Illinois, and that's where I wanted to be.

But the coaching staff wanted me to pay my dues. I could feel it. I was talented, but not enough for them to overlook the guys they sought after, recruited, and were paying for in big scholarship dollars.

I remember my running-back coach saying to me once: "You're a young pup. And young pups don't get to play."

So I waited my turn.

"They're messing me around . . . they're holding me back."

I was actually having a good time. The guys on the team were tight. I was hanging out with Henry Jones, Mike Bellamy, Quintin Parker, Darrick Brownlow, and Frank Hartley. I also had some buddies there who were so upset about not playing, they wanted to transfer schools. They were all in my ear:

"You need to be playing. You know man, you need to transfer and come down to Missouri. We're all going to Missouri."

I think one of the former coaches who recruited them was at Missouri at the time. They wanted me to go down there so we could all play together. If I remember correctly, one of the guys got the chance to play, but the other one, the running back, went down there and never made it on the field.

I must admit, I was tempted. But I had this gut feeling about Illinois. I just knew that one day I'd get my chance.

I used to call Coach Smith back in

GRIFF NOTE: *Distractions can get your off your game.*

Chicago so he could help me work through my frustration. I'd pick up the phone in a minute and tell him: "They're messing me around…. they're holding me back."

Then he would jump in his car and make the two-hour drive to Champaign to see what was happening. He wanted to know for himself. Coach Smith would always talk to me about the behind-the-scenes bureaucracy that goes on at universities, which helped me calm down. But I wanted to play.

I was especially frustrated my second year because we were playing so poorly. I remember once, head coach Mike White put a scab offense together. This was the year of the NFL strike, so Coach White was trying to do something to keep the team motivated. He took freshman and

"When is all this going to pay off?"

sophomore special-teams players and developed an offense called the "scab offense." He'd say, "I'm telling you, if the offense sputters, you guys are going to be out there." He would get us all psyched up, making us think we were going to have a chance to play. So we'd be out there playing hard, just waiting for one of the regular guys to mess up. Of course, we never got in. Come game day, we'd be sitting on the sideline.

Don't get me wrong. We had some talented recruits, but I still felt that I had something to bring to the table.

I often asked myself: *When is it all going to pay off?*

Too much contemplation, however, left me drained and tired, so I tried hard to concentrate and wait patiently. I knew it was going to take time to reach the top of my game, but it felt like so much time had passed since I first joined the team.

Finally, I came to the conclusion that I had no control over when I'd have a big breakthrough. None of us do. All we can do is keep it moving.

Whenever I had doubts or reservations about my talent or ability to play at the level that was expected, I'd think back to my senior year of high school. Then I'd revisit my game plan. I had taken a chance on myself. I believed I was good enough, that I had what it took.

Whether the people at Illinois knew it or not, I was their guy.

And I was getting better all the time.

SIDELINE

Bucky Godbolt,
Former Illinois Offensive Coordinator

"I knew right away that Howard had all the skills. And he was an intelligent football player. I don't know what his classroom situation was. It is kind of hard to tell what a Prop 48 guy is. All you know is that when you sit there and have discussions with Howard, you can tell the intelligence is there."

"He was a smart guy on the field. He can go to a playbook and read the plays and he'll know the play after you talk about it one time. He doesn't have to go on and on and on. The only time he has to do repetition is on the field. But when you say this is the play, this is the design, he visualizes that. He can visualize that in a classroom, where, with other guys, you have to walk through it. You have to show it to them. He analyzes things really well and really quickly."

As far as I was concerned, I was a competitor, and during that time, we weren't playing well, which meant we needed to be playing the best people on the squad. I felt I could have made a difference on the team. Even if I wasn't a starter, I knew I had something to contribute to the offense. All I needed was the opportunity.

GRIFF NOTES

Throughout my years of playing football, one of the things I have enjoyed most is the quality of the relationships you develop in a team atmosphere. You learn from them. And if you're open, you can grow in leaps and bounds. Team dynamics force you to step up to the plate and take a closer look at yourself—which is a good thing. It is because of the respect and admiration I have for my teammates that I am encouraged to go out and play to the best of my ability— not sometimes, but every time.

Keep in mind that your primary purpose on the team is to contribute your talents and abilities to the overall game plan. Consider the following suggestions, which may help you on a personal level to interact more efficiently in a team situation:

• Follow your better judgment.

Your gut feeling is not to be ignored. When you believe in an action, idea, or issue, pursue it. You may need reinforcements (i.e., additional research, support materials, the advice of a higher authority), but continue pursuing what you feel is right. If you make a strong-enough case, you may get others to see things your way.

- **Stick to the game plan.**

Investigate all avenues of a given plan so that you understand fully what your responsibility is in the execution of the plan.

- **Respect the team's legacy.**

Upon joining a team, respect the groundwork that has been laid by members who have already put in the time and effort necessary to bring the team to its present status.

- **Make necessary adjustments.**

Once a plan of action has been set into motion, monitor the results. If you find that it's not working, make the necessary adjustments immediately. The sooner you acknowledge that there's an area of weakness, the sooner you can address it and sustain more profitable results.

- **Set a disciplined work ethic.**

Productivity is a priority. Ensure that your time is being put to good use. In addition to the set team schedules, set individual routines for yourself that allow you to be better prepared once team play begins. This strategy keeps you fresh and on your toes, so that you're ready for any given situation.

- **Utilize every opportunity.**

When you find yourself underutilized or working in an area that's not particularly your field area of expertise, find creative ways to capitalize on the job you're currently doing. Make good use of every opportunity you're afforded. The knowledge you gain could be immeasurable in the future.

- **Distractions can get you off your game.**

When you turn your attention away from the game and your responsibility as a player, you are distracted. No matter what form they come in—as events, circumstances, or setbacks—distractions creep up from out of nowhere and try to beat you at your game. Stay alert. Dismiss distractions as inconsequential occurrences, address them immediately, and place them in their proper perspective—low on the ladder of priorities and unnecessary for the completion of your set goals.

- **Be productive during down periods.**

In the off-season, remain productive. Find ways to stay on your toes, to investigate new opportunities, to study an area outside of your comfort zone. Keep learning and growing during slow periods or periods where your input isn't essential, so during the season, you're more prepared than ever.

—Trust in your ability as well as your teammates' ability to accomplish set goals.

—For team leaders, cover your bases in terms of each player's skills and abilities. Make sure that everyone on your team is up to the task at hand.

—Ask yourself what it is that you can contribute in order to maintain balance within the group or organization.

3   THE DRILL

IN THE COLLEGE MEDIA GUIDES, I remember reading about all of the great Illinois players—their stats, their claims to fame. This is how I stayed motivated while playing for a coaching staff that was not completely convinced of my ability.

It was a long two years, waiting to play, but in the spring of 1989, I became the starting fullback. Coach John Mackovic joined the team that year as well, replacing Mike White as head coach. I was finally on the field, wearing jersey No. 29.

Time to execute the game plan.

The Fighting Illini had well-established standards that all of their players upheld. I was expected to do the same. The pressure had been turned up a few more notches.

GRIFF NOTE: *Adjust to new leadership.*

In the beginning, making the adjustment from Mike White to John Mackovic was dif-

ficult. Coach Mack came in like gangbusters, with a totally different coaching style, a chip on his shoulder, and plenty of ideas about
where he wanted the team to go. Though he was a tough taskmas-
ter, we didn't think he had taken the time to get to know his players.
As a result, there was a hostility and tension in the organization that
hadn't existed before.

SIDELINE

Coach John Mackovic,
Former Illinois Head Coach

"I didn't know much about Howard when I first arrived because I came in the very beginning of February, and the
recruiting season had been over. There was an abrupt
change in the coaching pattern there. So, I didn't get the
chance to know any of the players for several weeks. We
were trying to put our team together that spring. We had
a young man, Keith Jones, who emerged as our starting
tailback. And Howard worked his way in—we weren't sure
where to play him—but we wanted to get our two best
backs on the field. He ended up being our fullback. I didn't
really know much about him because he didn't really stand

out, necessarily. He did what we asked him to do, and he practiced hard, but he didn't stand out. He wasn't alone. I think players were trying to learn our system and get familiar with it, and it was difficult for them to show their best."

SIDELINE

Henry Jones
Defensive Back, Buffalo Bills

"I met Howard our freshman year. I really didn't know what to expect, and when I got to training camp, I was shocked by the level of conditioning and the competition, I was not prepared. It took me a couple of years to get adjusted mentally and physically. At first, I didn't like Coach Mackovic, I thought he was too prudish and besides, I was recruited by Mike White, and I wanted to play for him. I was biased. But after we started winning, it didn't matter to me that Mackovic was the coach. I accepted him."

"I realized what he was trying to do was discipline us."

SIDELINE

Quintin Parker,
Former Illinois Strong Safety

"Initially, I didn't think much of Coach Mackovic at all. I thought he was on a power trip and that he really didn't understand any of us. After about a year, I realized, 'Man, he *does* understand. He *really* knows what he's doing.' I realized later that what he was trying to do was discipline us."

SIDELINE

Mike Bellamy,
Former Illinois Wide Receiver/
Former Philadelphia Eagle

"John Mackovic wasn't our favorite person when he first got there. He was trying to turn us into men and wouldn't allow us to be the immature boys that we were. Well, we didn't appreciate that . . . not until much later. We thought he was pushing us too hard. But in the end, we all respected him."

SIDELINE

Coach John Mackovic,
Former Illinois Head Coach

"I've always believed that coaching is teaching. The most important part of working with a team is teaching them how to do the best they can do, and then giving them the opportunity to learn how to be successful through any number of different motivational means—driving them to be the best that they can be. I think a lot of times football is best characterized by coaches who drive their teams to be better than they might have been. It is a difficult game. It requires a great deal of discipline. To achieve a level of success, some football coaches, traditionally, have pushed people to work harder than they'd be willing to work on their own. And I clearly would put myself in that category. I was not afraid to do that."

When I started playing, my father and my stepmother, Joy, would come down to every single game, even away games. I had friends back home who would follow every game on television. They knew I had been working hard for a long time to get my chance out on the field.

Coach Smith came down often to watch practices. In fact, he made it a habit to check on his former players, no matter where they were. Corwin Brown, now with the Detroit Lions, was at Michigan at that time, so Coach would check in with him, then swing back and visit me in Champaign. Even when guys made it to the pros, he would go to training camps to see how they were doing. It's his paternal nature. He's now the Athletic Director of Chicago Public Schools. But, I suppose, once a coach always a coach.

In a game against Utah, I had the chance I had been waiting for my entire college career. It was an unforgettable game.

I had a 76-yard run.

I started to the left and kept cutting back like inside of 10 yards. I kept making guys miss; then I ran down the sideline into the end zone. My performance caught the attention of the sports media, and from that point forward, the local press paid close attention to my career.

Also, I had made an impressive showing to the Illini coaching staff. The Utah game was a proving ground. It was an opportunity to start in an important game and put my skills to the test.

My desire to win often sent my temper into high gear.

After that game, Coach Mackovic began to take notice.

One of the things I'll always respect about the Illinois organization is its insistence that every player be proud. I knew that I wasn't just wearing the uniform for myself, but for all of the guys who came before me—guys like Hall of Famer Bobby Mitchell, J.C. Caroline, Dick Butkus, Ray Nitschke, and Jim Grabowski.

The Illinois legacy is impressive.

Learning the Illini history was considered as important as learning game plays. We understood, early on, that for any team to succeed, there must be a measure of respect *for* the team and *among* the team. It was this foundation that helped me put things into perspective early in my career and develop the mind-set of a team player.

In game after game, my performance spoke for itself. I started making progress, delivering on my promise to make a difference on the team. And I quickly became a valued and respected player. My teammates and coaches could sense my determination and commitment to the team.

I wanted to win.

But my desire to win often sent my temper into high gear.

Illinois vs. Iowa

At that time, we had one of the best defenses in the country. And Iowa's defense was ranked pretty high as well. Our defensive

coordinator, Lou
Tepper, had an out-
standing record. So
we knew, going in,
that any team we

GRIFF NOTE: *Keep your attitude in check.*

played would have a difficult time scoring against us.

By halftime, we were killing them. I probably had 50 rushing yards and 34 receiving yards. I was playing well. Then, in the third quarter, the ball was thrown in the dirt, and this young player, an outside linebacker, decided to run behind me and push me. So without hesitating, I turned around and slapped him.

"Griffith, you're out of here!" the official shouted.

SIDELINE

Mike Bellamy,
Former Illinois Wide Receiver/
Former Philadelphia Eagle

"Howard is a very intense guy, and that was an intense game. We were a confident team. And when Howard dropped that ball, he was so mad at himself. He is the epitome of a team player, and whenever he drops a ball, he feels that he has let his team down. He felt like he hadn't done his part. And he takes his job very seriously. Then, when that linebacker pushed him late—he was really up-set. He was not going to allow that guy to embarrass him any further. He was upset enough that he had dropped the ball. So his reaction was more out of frustration from dropping the ball than it was from the push. It didn't mat-ter what Mike Bellamy felt, it didn't matter what Quintin Parker felt, or John Mackovic, or what his parents felt. Howard felt that he had let his team down, which is the last thing in the world he wants to do."

At that time in my career, I hadn't mastered the art of main-taining my focus for an entire game. In spite of how hard I worked during practice—running the drills, studying plays, knowing my position—I was prone to letting my emotions take over which cost me in the end.

Coach Mackovic didn't say much about the incident. He just gave me that look.

I recalled a conversation I had with him when he first joined the team. We didn't get along at all. He was very disciplined and expected only the best from his players. It was during one of our first meetings; he came in, pointed me out, and said: "Howard, there have been three negative incidents on the team this season, and you've been involved in two of them."

He was referring to my temper. He told me: "Look, I know you don't like me, but I don't like you either…not the way you're acting. But if you're going to play on my team, you're going to do things *my* way."

Coach Mackovic wanted the best for all of us. He knew we could be better players and better students. In fact, around this time, many of us were suffering academically, so Coach came up with a name for us. He called us "The Dirty Thirteen."

SIDELINE

Mike Bellamy,
Former Illinois Wide Receiver/
Former Philadelphia Eagle

"Coach John Mackovic and Mike Hatfield, the academic advisor, came up with that name for us—'the dirty thirteen.' It wasn't because we were ruthless or outsiders, but we needed guidance. It came about because some of the guys would get in trouble, you know, just being in the wrong place at the wrong time. And each time, it was like 'Here we go again.' But we needed time to mature. You're talking about 18- and 19-year-old kids. Coach Mack would tell us: 'I'm not being negative. I'm being positive…and I'm positive that you all are not going to be here.' Well, that presented the challenge. It was a defining moment in my life.

We all took what he said about us personally. And then we got the attitude of, 'OK, just watch me.'

"Think about it. We were kids with two jobs. We had to wake up early, take class at a major university. It wasn't easy. None of us were expected to do half the things we have achieved. You're talking about going to a predominantly white school, getting your education from this all-white school...we weren't expected to succeed. But all of us did. We all graduated and got our degrees. It was a learning ground for us.

"The football experience at Illinois was an excellent opportunity for us to mature. All of us, the so-called "dirty thirteen" in that group, are successful today."

SIDELINE

Coach John Mackovic,
Former Illinois Head Coach

"The Dirty Thirteen were all players who had done very poorly academically. It wasn't a matter of them doing poorly, then I showed up, and everybody turned into Cinderella. They weren't doing very well. So we had what I called a 'come to Jesus' meeting, and I told them that it didn't matter to me whether any of them made it or not, that we were going to demand certain things of them. If they lived up to them, great, but if they didn't, they would not be there. It basically had to do with academics. And I think Howard would admit, and several others, that when they went to college, they might not have ever really thought or expected to graduate. They wanted to be athletes. They dreamed of being in the National Football League. And playing college football was certainly an avenue for that, and part of that dream. But whether or not they got a college education or a degree was probably secondary. And from my standpoint, education had to be just as important as playing football."

GRIFF NOTE: *Take responsibility for your actions.*

Though I had an outstanding season my junior year, because of my outbursts and unsportsmanlike conduct on the field, my coaches stopped pushing me for postseason honors.

Their message was clear: Undisciplined behavior would not be tolerated.

I was playing with great athletes like Jeff George, Mo Gardner, Henry Jones, Chris Green, Mel Agee, Steven Williams, Mike

Bellamy, Sean Streeter, Quintin Parker, and Darrick Brownlow. We had an incredible team roster. So I wasn't about to compromise my position on the team because of my attitude.

I got with the program and straightened up my act.

That same year, we made it to the Michigan game with a chance to win the Big Ten title.

Illinois vs. Michigan

As a team, we wanted the Big Ten title. We had worked hard all year, and we desperately wanted to win a national championship as well. But oddly enough, Coach Mack took a different approach to the game. He said: "It's a regular game. We're just as good as they are. Let's just go out and play." He was surprisingly laid back. So instead of tightening up our game plan, devising winning strategies, and running new drills, we went through our normal practice routine. We treated a potential national championship game like any other game.

SIDELINE

**Quintin Parker,
Former Illinois Strong Safety**

"Coach Mackovic's approach was to treat it like 'a normal game.' Don't treat the game any differently, he told us.

But, hey, Michigan *was* different. I think *he* made the mistake—not us. It was for the Big Ten championship! Probably the biggest game of our college careers."

GRIFF NOTE: *Never underestimate the competition.*

While it was exciting to be a part of a possible Big Ten championship, we weren't ready. We wanted to win, but we went in with serious doubts, and it showed in our performance.

Plays that usually worked for us fell flat. We were struggling throughout the entire game. I remember one play in particular where we had the ball down on the 4-yard line, but we weren't able to convert and get it in for a touchdown. It might have been first-and-goal or second goal. So we ran a trick play. We were faking a play action pass that had worked for us in games before, but Michigan was playing zone defense. We didn't have a chance. They were right there and knocked the ball down.

It was a terrible loss. Everyone was disappointed—the coaches, the players, the fans, the university.

Coach Mack was devastated. He called a team meeting, and we all spoke openly about how passive our performance had been. What I realized, and expressed at the meeting, was

> **GRIFF NOTE:** *Offer constructive criticism.*

that our attitude and mentality was the same as our coach's. Coach Mack had a laid-back attitude, and that's how we went out and played that game. We laid back.

I made my opinion known and everyone listened. It was more important to me at that point to air my frustrations openly, in front of the entire team than to worry about the ramifications of directly criticizing the head coach. Now, he could have gotten mad at me for saying it, or made me run laps, even kicked me off the team, but instead, he agreed with me. And it changed our relationship. From that point on, our relationship was much closer. The positive outcome of a disappointing loss was the mutual respect and understanding that developed between Coach Mackovic and his team.

SIDELINE

Coach John Mackovic,
Former Illinois Head Coach

"Well, when you're a coach, it's always tough when things don't go as planned. Whether you run the ball or pass the

> ball, if it doesn't work, you stand open for criticism. I re-
> member Howard was very outspoken about it, not in a nega-
> tive way, but in a way that expressed that he wanted to be
> personally as good as he could be, and he wanted our team
> to be as good as it could be. And I listened to him."

Playing in the Big Ten was always unpredictable. There was just no way of knowing which team was going to step up to the forefront. So often, you'd go in thinking you were going to waste a team, then you'd have an off day or that opponent would be super-motivated, and next thing you know, you've lost to a team you assumed you'd beat easily.

Michigan was on top. The Wolverines had a powerhouse team, and then the following year, it was Iowa with the great team.

By my senior year, we had made some huge achievements as a team. Illinois had lived up to all of my original expectations. I had received the kind of press I had hoped for, and had gotten the attention from NFL scouts.

It was the ultimate college football experience.

One game that stands out in my mind as one of the most meaningful in my college career was against Colorado. At the time, the Buffaloes were the No. 1 college football team in the country. No one expected us to win, because Colorado was a top-ranked

GRIFF NOTE: *It takes a total team effort.*

team and had gone through their whole season undefeated. We, on the other hand, had recently lost to Arizona, a team we were predicted to beat.

It was an intense game. We were falling far behind and had to come back to win it. It took a total team effort. But our ultimate victory told the story of how good a team we had become. Although Colorado won the national championship that year, we had successfully ended their undefeated status, representing the only blemish on their record for the season.

SIDELINE

Quintin Parker,
Former Illinois Strong Safety

"The Colorado game was probably the most telling tale of our college experience. We had played a lot of supposedly great teams, but at the time, Colorado was one of the top teams in the country. We had already lost to Arizona—who we were supposed to beat. But in the Colorado game,

> I remember we were down in that game, then came back
> and won it. They gave Howard the ball and let him do his
> thing."

Headlines

"Frantic Illini Roller-Coaster Stops at Top," by Robert
Markus. (Reprinted from the *Chicago Tribune*, September 16, 1990):

*"In a game with more twists and turns than an Agatha Christie
plot, Illinois finally solved the mystery of Colorado's option attack and
gained redemption Saturday.*

*The vaunted Illinois defense, riddled in an opening loss last week
at Arizona, was magnificent in the second half as the Illini rallied for a
nail-biting 23-22 victory over the nation's ninth-ranked team.*

*The 21-ranked Illini thus exorcised the memory of last year's 38-
7 bashing at Colorado, which had haunted them for a year.*

*'I think our defense had a lot to prove,' defensive coordinator Lou
Tepper said. 'They wanted to regain their respect as a national-caliber
team, and I think they did that.'*

*They punctuated a sterling performance by stopping Colorado
cold in the final minute after [quarterback Jason] Verduzco had directed a 63-yard fourth-quarter drive for the winning touchdown. Senior co-captain Howard Griffith scored it with 1:18 to play on a one-
yard drive, capping a day that was as up-and-down for him personally
as it was for the team.*

*Griffith led Illinois with 90 rushing yards, including a 45-yard
burst down the sideline that set up the touchdown that tied the score at
17. But he also was nailed in the end zone just moments later for a
safety that returned the lead to Colorado at 19-17. Griffith thought he*

had escaped the end zone when he was submarined by Colorado line-backer Greg Biekert.

'But I guess it was a blessing in disguise,' he said, 'because it caused us to suck it up and get the job done.'

———————————

In my final season, all the hard work, humility, diligence, patience, and perseverance culminated in one unforgettable, remarkable career accomplishment, which I never saw coming. In the fall of 1990, a single game would signify my greatest collegiate achievement. It went down like this:

We were playing Southern Illinois, our rivals from downstate, and we believed that we could blow them out. But they had other plans. We looked up in the second quarter and the score was 21-

"I could see the frustration on everyone's face."

0. Southern was on top. I was directly responsible for one of those touchdowns, after one of the Saluki linebackers came and ripped the ball out of my arms and ran it in for a touchdown.

We were fumbling for answers.

Coach Mack was going berserk!

We were getting ready to start the Big Ten season the following week. In practice, he had been pressing us to go in and get this done, to get the season off to a great start.

I could see the frustration on everyone's face. It was a bleak scene. But we regained our focus and came up with an alternate game plan that we hoped would turn things around.

At the moment Southern thought they had it all wrapped up, the momentum of the game shifted in our favor.

I ran in for three touchdowns in the second quarter, helping us close Southern's lead.

Then, in the final minutes before the half, our defense forced a turnover that gave us the ball back. Bucky Godbolt, our running-back coach said to me: "We're going to run a 39-toss. Do you want to run it?"

My first reply was, "Man, I'm kinda tired."

He said, "Go ahead and take it."

So I went for it and ran the ball in for a 51-yard touchdown. The team was hyped, the crowd went crazy, and it was the play we needed to get ourselves back on track.

Finally, we were ahead.

After that touchdown, it seemed like every time I touched the ball I was running into the end zone. At halftime, the buzz started in the locker room about the legendary Illini running back, Red Grange, and his 1924 record. The media even started digging through the archives to figure out just how close I was to breaking his record.

Red's record was 32 career touchdowns and five touchdowns in a single collegiate game. He scored five TDs and passed on trying for a sixth in a game against Michigan. Now, here I was, 66 years later, on my way to breaking his long-standing record. It was an incredible prospect.

The talk continued on the sideline and it just wouldn't stop. I remember telling Coach Mack, "Listen, we don't have to keep doing this." But he said: "Hey, when you're this close…it's not like we're trying to go in and blow this team out, but this is something special that you will always cherish. You'll thank me for this years from now."

He wanted me to go for the NCAA record.

I went for it.

I tied Red's record with five touchdowns by the third quarter. And by the end of the game, I had surpassed the NCAA record of seven touchdowns in a game by scoring eight touchdowns in a single game.

SIDELINE

Kim Griffith,
Howard's wife

"I will never forget that game against Southern. I rode down to Champaign with Howard's parents, and as far as we were concerned, it was just another college game. We had no idea what was in store. Also, at that time, I didn't know as much about football as I do now. All I really knew was that when you run the ball into the end zone, it's a touchdown. Well, every time I looked up, Howard had the ball and was headed for the end zone. It was crazy. Everybody in the stands was going berserk. His parents and I were beside ourselves. We couldn't believe what was happening. After the third touchdown, we calmed down a little and thought: 'Oh, what a great game Howard had.' Then, he started up again. The scoreboard looked like it was in constant motion. He was in rare form. After the sixth, the seventh, and finally the eighth touchdown, I thought I was going to faint. I had been screaming so loud throughout the game that my voice was gone. I was in tears, and I just remember being more excited than I had ever been. We waited for Howard as always to come out of the locker room; but after that game, it took the longest it had ever taken him to come out. The press was all over him. When we made it back to his apartment, the phones were ringing off the hook. Every major newspaper, radio station, and television network was calling him. It was an incredible day."

There are no words to describe that moment. It was an unbelievable rush. To this day, people who were at that game come up to me and want to talk about it. It was an *amazing* game.

SIDELINE

Bucky Godbolt,
Former Illinois Running Back Coach

"I was told by somebody when Howard first got there, 'Well, don't worry. This guy is probably not going to make it. He won't make it academically, and he probably won't be around so don't waste your time with him. Well, he went on to graduate, become one of the all-time great players in Illinois history, scored more touchdowns in Illini history than anybody in a single game. So, he has proved everybody wrong. And he continues to do that now. He just continues to do it. That's how he is."

The press went crazy. There was a media frenzy with more hype than I could have ever imagined. I was doing radio and television interviews, and offers for public appearances were coming in regularly. I remember we had the following week off, but because of the frenzy, I had a hard time preparing for the upcoming game. I couldn't get that game out of my head, and my teammates remained excited about it during the weeks that followed.

SIDELINE

Mike Bellamy,
Former Illinois Wide Receiver/
Former Philadelphia Eagle

"I didn't get to see that game against Southern because I was in my first year in the NFL and I was in practice. Well, guys started coming over to me, saying, 'Man, your boy did this . . . and your boy did that.' They knew that I was a close friend of Howard's. Then my mother called. And my father called. Everybody back in Chicago was telling me about what happened. It was really important to me. I remember watching ESPN. They'd show a picture of Red Grange and a picture of Howard...a picture of Red, then a picture of Howard. It was so exciting. But it's true, nobody expected him to do it, nobody wanted him to do it. So they decided not to respect it. It wasn't looked at as being the huge accomplishment that it was. But Howard was just out there proving himself. He proved another point: 'I told you this is what I was capable of.' He had an 'I told you so,' attitude. And it was great for all of us, especially all those guys on the Illinois team who were from Chicago."

It brought to mind all of the years of hard work—the struggles, the trials, the sweat and tears. It was the kind of experience that brings about several emotions, all at the same time. You don't know whether to laugh, cry, shout, or holler. Everything comes so close to the surface—from the C you got in political science because you stayed up all night going over the game plan for Saturday's game, to the look in your father's eye the first time he saw you hit a home run in Little League. It was simply overwhelming.

And it was the opportunity of a lifetime.

SIDELINE

Coach John Mackovic,
Former Illinois Head Coach

"After Keith Jones left, we were trying to figure out how we would go forward. Howard became more instrumental in our plan. We were beginning to see what he could do. It was during that season when he busted loose, running for eight touchdowns in one game, that really put him not only in the record books at Illinois and in the record books of college football, but it really was the signal by him that we could count on him to be our big playmaker, that he was willing to take that role and accept the leadership position as our team runner."

GRIFF NOTE: *Individual accomplishment equals team accomplishment.*

Breaking the NCAA record was an accomplishment that no other back in the league could claim. When people hear about the eight touchdowns, they assume that they were all one-yard, "dive into the end zone" kind of plays. But they weren't. Our entire team played well that day, and the payoff was big.

Though I could not have done it without my teammates, it was a personal success story that I'm now able to tuck away that can never be taken away from me. It's an experience that lives with you, that you can draw upon whenever you need it.

That's one of the great things about playing on a team. There are moments when everyone has his or her turn for personal glory. We went into that game with the expectation of winning, and when things turned against us, we knew we'd have to step up. Everyone had to rise to the occasion. No one went into that game thinking: "We're going to give Howard eight touchdowns." No one, including me, ever thought that was even possible. But the end results benefited the whole organization.

GRIFF NOTE: *Unselfishness pays.*

Part of team play is knowing when to pass the ball, when to make the way for someone else to score. It's being an unselfish player. Without camaraderie, a team dies. I'll always credit my college teammates and coaches for their support, assistance, and encouragement. They helped make a great player out of me, not only in that game against Southern but throughout my college football career.

The Red Grange experience didn't end there. There were still some other barriers to hurdle. I found out, soon after the game, that there were a significant number of fans, critics, and former players who felt that Red's record should have never been touched. I started hearing rumblings about disgruntled fans who were disgusted with the whole thing and who blamed Coach Mackovic for allowing it to happen.

Red Grange was and always will be an Illini hero. He meant so much to the university and to the game of football. And my breaking his record was considered by some an insult, or at least an act of blatant disrespect.

SIDELINE

Quintin Parker,
Former Illinois Strong Safety

"What's amazing about Howard breaking Red Grange's record is that he hasn't gotten enough credit for what he did. Most people don't realize that we were losing that game to Southern Illinois. And our defense at the time was ranked in the top 10, and there we were, losing to a smaller school. Basically, Mack was like, 'Hey, if we can't run the ball and win this game, I'd rather lose.' So he put the pressure on Howard . . . and Howard took the game over! I don't think he has gotten enough credit for scoring eight touchdowns in a single game. There were people who didn't want *any* comparisons made between Howard and Red Grange. Red Grange was such a sports icon. In many ways, he started professional football by himself, in addition to having a great college career. So, Howard's great achievement was downplayed.

"It would make a great trivia question: 'Who holds the record for most touchdowns in a single game in the NCAA?' I bet money, people would start naming all kinds of players—Barry Sanders, Emmitt Smith—who were great college players, but they didn't do what Howard did. I'm sure people would name everybody in the world, except Howard Griffith...but that's all right, I'll win money on that bet."

Later in the season, we played in the Hall of Fame Bowl down in Tampa. Mike Pearson, who was in charge of the Sports Information Department at Illinois, had this idea that Red Grange and I should meet. Red lived 45 minutes from where we'd be playing in Indian Lake Estates, Florida.

Mike said: "Howard, we have some great ideas for you. It's the 100th year of Illini football. It started with Grange and now it's come full circle with you. So we want to do a Grange/Griffith kind of thing."

So he set it up.

I felt good about the meeting. It would be a privilege, I thought. I felt like an ambassador for the university. And I also thought it would put to rest all of the hoopla that had surrounded the whole thing and would possibly appease the people who had gotten upset over it.

SIDELINE

Mike Pearson,
Former Illinois Sports Information Director

"Once the bowl bid was made to the University of Illinois in early December, I immediately contacted Mrs. Grange and asked if it would be possible, once we arrived in Tampa, to drive Howard over to meet Red, due to all of the historical events concerning Howard and Red that season. Because Red was in intensive care in a small hospital in Lake Wales, Florida, Mrs. Grange flatly said no, the first time. Then, a couple of days before we left Champaign for Tampa, I received a call from Mrs. Grange. She said that she'd reconsidered and that she'd like Howard to be able to meet Red.

Honestly, I can't remember when I told Howard about this visit, but he was very excited about the possibility of meeting the man whose records he had broken. When we arrived at the hospital, Red was extremely weak, and frankly, I wasn't very hopeful that he would even realize who we were.

"I remember saying, 'Mr. Grange, I want to introduce you to Howard Griffith. This is the young man who has broken all of your records this past season at the University of Illinois.' After about 10 to 15 seconds of silence, Mr. Grange still hadn't responded, and I was resigned to the fact that he didn't understand anything I'd said. Then, in a very faint voice, Red said, 'Oh, I know who Howard is.' I immediately turned to Howard and saw this terrific smile on his face. They shook hands, and I knew that this would be a moment Howard and I would never forget.

"About a month later, Red died. I thank God these two Illini legends had a chance to meet."

I'll never forget the day I met Red Grange.

As soon as we came out of practice that day, I barely had time to shower before I had to head down to meet Red. His wife, Margaret, who everyone called, "Muggs," had agreed to the meeting. She met us at the doors of the retirement home. She was friendly and clearly excited about us being there. That day, she gave me a stuffed doll that she had knitted in the orange and blue Illini colors. (I still have it sitting on my trophy shelf.) She told me right away how proud Red was of our team and my recent accomplishment. She also mentioned that she had been reading the recent press clippings to Red, and they both had kept up with my career. This news shocked me. I had no idea. I didn't even think Red Grange knew who I was until the game against Southern. Muggs told me that Red was impressed with my record and knew how hard I had worked to come up through the ranks.

But believe it or not, even after it became a well-known fact that Red was pleased with my NCAA record, there were still those members of the "old guard" who said it was reprehensible. And I'd *I'll never forget the day I met Red Grange.* be lying if I said that I didn't think racism didn't play a part in all of the opposition. I mean, Red represented for some people a "great white hope." So "Who is this black kid from the South Side who thinks he's bad enough to break his record?"

Nevertheless, Red was thrilled, and so was I.

During that time, Red, over 90 years old, was in poor health. When we walked into his room, he acknowledged me with a head nod. He couldn't speak much, but a nod was good enough for me.

I was in awe of him, and it was an extraordinary experience just being in his presence.

I mean, he was the "Galloping Ghost."

Red Grange had brought people in the stands. He was the most closely watched athlete of his day. He was the guy people wanted to see turn pro, which he did immediately after graduating from Illinois. Fans flocked to the stadium to see him play for the Chicago Bears, paying an admission price to see professional sports for the first time in our history.

In fact, there was so much hype surrounding him, in his first season of professional ball, he played 18 games in a two- or three-month period. The whole country wanted to see him, so they set it up so fans could watch him play with regularity. They had him playing as much as was physically possible. He was a star running back and one of America's first "celebrity" athletes.

Who didn't want to be another Red Grange?

I certainly wanted the chance. But what I had confirmed for myself in those years at Illinois was the power of belief. Performing well both athletically and academically was a major feat for me. After the fact, I realized that the trials and challenges were invaluable, and the real goal was to come out of the other side victorious, having learned some valuable lessons—lessons I could take with me to get to the next step.

GRIFF NOTES

What Is the Drill?

A drill is an activity that is practiced over and over again until it becomes a natural and integral part of your overall game plan.

As a fullback, one of the drills I practice regularly is catching the ball. I don't get an opportunity to catch a lot of balls in a game, but when they come my way, it's important that I *make* the catch— whether it's an easy catch or a tough catch. In a drill exercise, you become so accustomed to the activity that you can be assured of a measure of success on game day.

Running a drill requires persistence and a thorough understanding of its importance in the overall scheme of things. A drill is nothing more than what we all learned in elementary school: Practice makes perfect.

Other Aspects to Support the Drill:

- ### Keep your attitude in check

There are occasions when maintaining a level head is absolutely necessary but nearly impossible to achieve. However, it gets back to focus. The more focused you are, the less likely you are to lose control in stressful situations.

• Adjust to new leadership

Everyone needs transition time whenever a change in the team dynamic takes place. While changing leaders is unsettling, it doesn't have to be disruptive. Communication is the key here—listening to the ideas the new leader has for the team and sharing your thoughts and feelings with him about where the team stands on certain issues.

• Take responsibility for your actions

Each player is responsible for his or her own behavior. Players must keep in mind that their actions are a reflection on the entire team.

• Never underestimate the competition

Underestimating another team or competitor immediately puts you at a disadvantage. This attitude makes you vulnerable and will likely cost you in the end.

- ## Offer constructive criticism

An interchange between teammates is healthy. And it is important that every player feels that he or she has a voice. Constructive criticism only makes others on your team aware of a possible roadblock ahead, a weak link, an area of weakness that if addressed, can be rectified. Proper protocol is that individual or personal matters are taken up in private, and matters that affect the whole team are addressed to the whole team.

- ## It takes a total team effort

Every win requires a total team effort. Everyone must step up and do their part. This never changes. The whole idea of a team is one unit moving together to accomplish a collective goal.

- ## Individual accomplishment equals team accomplishment

Individual performance should not be separated from team performance. When your personal efforts have contributed greatly to the team's set goal, the whole team wins.

•   **Unselfishness pays**

Selfishness, gloating, and self-importance alienate other players. A team atmosphere should make everyone feel that his or her role is an important and necessary part of the whole. Being an unselfish player is being a team player.

BY THE TIME I GRADUATED FROM THE UNIVERSITY OF ILLINOIS with a bachelor of arts degree in speech/communications, I was one of the top players on the Illini football team. When the NFL draft came around, I was expected to do well.

Despite some minor concerns, I didn't have any doubt that I'd be drafted in the NFL. I just didn't know what round. I had a productive college career. I had put in the time, done the work. So, I approached the draft with a great deal of confidence.

I expected good results.

SIDELINE

Randall Townsel,
Friend/Former Julian Football Player

"I never gave it a second thought— Howard being drafted? It wasn't a question of: 'Will he be drafted?' It was only a question of 'Which round?'"

The NFL combine in Indianapolis, where the top 300 college players go to be seen by NFL recruiters, is the ultimate meat market. They give you a hotel room, a roommate, and a shirt with an ID number. It's a weeklong event, and the players are usually there for about three days, separated into categories according to position. During that time, you are tested on your body, your mind, your reflexes, your speed, your strength, and your personality.

Fortunately, it's a once-in-a-lifetime event. It is an experience you won't forget, and one you definitely wouldn't want to repeat. While you're going through it, you feel like your whole life depends on the outcome.

Preparing for the combines, you don't know whether you need to be heavier in the workouts, or lighter. You're trying to run faster, tighten up your game, anything to try to give yourself an edge to gain the attention of the scouts. Winning the scouts over is always a trip because they usually have their own opinions about how a player should look and play. It affects your value and your ranking. And the scouts' opinions strongly influence a team's final decision.

> *While you're going through it, you feel like your whole life depends on it.*

To tell the truth, I wasn't sure of my role at this point. I was still holding on to the hope that I'd be a halfback. I talked to some of the scouts, and they weren't sure how I'd fit into the mix.

Coming into the combine, I had just returned from playing in the 1991 Hula Bowl. I put in a solid performance playing on the East team. I don't recall my stats, but the East beat the West in a tight game. Prob-lem was, word had begun to circulate

To tell the truth, I wasn't sure of my role at this point.

that I wasn't big enough to play in the pros. The general opinion was that I was talented but didn't have the size that some critics felt was needed. I wasn't the size of the prototypical full back or half-back. So there was some uncertainty about my overall potential.

That was the main challenge I faced—fitting into the defini-tion of a "typical" back. Weight-wise I was in an in-between area. There was a new trend evolving. Most teams wanted a fullback who was 6'2," 240 pounds. Because I was a little smaller than that, I didn't know where I'd fit in the mix. At the time, I must have weighed between 215 and 219. There was also the question of my speed. You are timed according to how fast you can run a 40-yard dash. A top speed is about 4.4 and under, 4.5 is considered average. My time was probably 4.7. The guys who were tailbacks coming out that year were running sub 4.4s and high 4.3s, and they were all around 5'9—Greg Lewis and Eric Bienemy types.

SIDELINE

Dr. J. W. Smith, Former Head Football Coach
Percy L. Julian High School

"Howard wasn't a halfback or a fullback in high school. He was a football player. If you asked him to block, he'd block. If you asked him to tackle, he'd tackle. If you asked him to run or catch, he'd do that. He'd do whatever you asked him to do. And with enthusiasm. Of all my players, Howard was the surest shot to make it big. Danny Walters was probably one of the greatest all-around athletes I've ever coached—so much natural ability. He went to Arkansas and was drafted by San Diego. He had the most potential, but not the motivation or resolve of Howard. You could just see the potential in Howard and his ability to wade through adversity and reach a goal. The thing about Howard was, he always carried himself in a manner that said, 'I'm separating myself. Don't mess with me.'"

Speed is still one of the biggest criteria for choosing backs. Most coaches figure the more speed a guy has, the bigger advantage he'll have on the field, which isn't always the case. I think more emphasis should be placed on what the guy did in college, how productive he was, as well as his overall character. Those elements will have a greater effect on a team in the long run, much more than whether a player runs 4.4 or 4.5.

In certain positions, like free safety for example, you take a guy who runs 4.4, 4.3, he is definitely going to be a higher draft than a safety who runs 4.6 because he can cover more field. If everything else is equal, the guy who is faster is going to be able to get the job done. However, if you have two guys who are equally fast, the guy who has a better knowledge of the game, who understands what is going on out there and can think on his feet, should be the guy who gets the job.

The problem is, qualities like good character, intelligence, and self-discipline are intangibles and rarely get the attention of the scouts. Nonetheless, they are the kind of traits that coaches will appreciate once the player makes the team.

The combine experience is unusual because you feel like cattle. You're herded around wearing a shirt with your number on it and your name. You go from room to room and wait your turn to be in-

"The thing about Howard was, he always carried himself in a manner that said, 'I'm separating myself. Don't mess with me.'"

terviewed. You're also given psychological tests, which you hope you're given early in the day, because by the end of the day, you're feeling half-crazy just for being there.

There you are lined up, waiting your turn, not knowing if you'll have great success or none at all. Going in, you're as prepared as you can possibly be, yet you're sitting next to guys who are Heisman Trophy candidates.

When you're waiting around, everybody's just looking at each other. Everybody's talking trash. It can be a fun time— nerve-wracking, but

No one ever forgets the combine experience.

fun. You get to meet a lot of great players. There were probably nine guys from the Illinois team there, so we were able to shake off some of our nerves together. Once you're in the NFL, you find yourself competing against guys you were in the combines with, and that's always a good time. It's like being a part of a small fraternity of players you've pledged with.

No one ever forgets the combine experience.

I remember seeing Russell Maryland, who grew up down the street from me in Chicago. He was being interviewed the first day I arrived at the combine. He was also my roommate at the Hula

Bowl. Then there were guys like Aaron Craver, a phenomenal athlete who, of course, was drafted high, and Nick Bell. We were all there together. I can remember being in the back room with them, warming up, getting ready to go run the 40, and there was Nick Bell, who was so big—at least 250 or 260—that the carpet was moving on his takeoffs. You could actually hear the carpet giving way when he started down the track.

The NFL draft takes place about six weeks after the combine. That particular year, it consisted of 12 rounds. At the time, there were some other star athletes I had competed with in all-star games who I figured would be drafted in the early rounds. Fullback Gerard Bunch of Michigan was selected in the first round, and Nick Bell of Iowa was drafted high in the second round.

Take Nick Bell for example—even with all that he had to offer, he didn't pan out the way the Raiders had planned. The Raiders thought he was going to be their star player. And while he had a few good years, he wasn't quite as stellar as they all had hoped. This is further proof that the drafting process is not an exact science. It's a hit-or-miss business, and much of the selection process is subjective and instinctive. Look at Terrell Davis, drafted in the sixth round; Shannon Sharpe, drafted in the later rounds; and Rod Smith, who wasn't drafted at all.

GRIFF NOTE: *Accentuate the positive.*

The interview was my strong suit. I gave strong interviews, but the problem was, I wasn't being requested by very many teams. I remember having good interviews with the New York Giants and the Cincinnati Bengals, but I wasn't able to talk to as many teams as I would have liked. And I figured it was a numbers game—the more people you talked to, the better your chances. So I made the best of it.

On draft day, I had been down in Carbondale at Southern Illinois University, partying at SpringFest. I was on my way home to Chicago, but I decided to stop in Champaign. I talked to my dad by phone, and he told me that some teams had been calling to speak to me. By this time, the draft had already started, so I knew I wasn't a fifth-round guy. I would have heard something sooner if I had been.

Day two, I got the call.

A coach's assistant called to say that I'd been picked up in the ninth round by the Indianapolis Colts, but I was asleep. I guess I sounded unenthusiastic, so they put Coach Ron Meyer on the line, and all I remember asking was:

"What round is it, anyway?"

I was slightly belligerent. I even remember saying, "Whatever, yeah, yeah, whatever…" The draft experience had gotten the best of me. I was tired at that point. I had put a lot of time and energy into the combines, and I could see the writing on the wall. I looked at all the running backs selected before me, and I wondered: *How in the world did that happen?*

I was disappointed. I expected my professional career to kick off with a bit more spark than it had. I had looked at all the guys who were at the combine, and I had expected to get a better reception. I thought my college stats would have counted for more. Being picked up in the ninth round was a big letdown.

And it got worse.

In 1991, I went to training camp at Indianapolis, which ended up being a huge waste of time. It didn't come as a surprise to me. I knew what kind of lineup the Colts had in place. Not only was running back Eric Dickerson coming back, in

"What round is it, anyway?"

a single-back set, but he was suddenly a happy camper, too. He'd been an angry man the preceding year; but apparently, all of his needs were being met and he had made peace with the organization over the off-season. So he was in good spirits and back to his normal work ethic.

In addition, Albert Bentley was at the top of his game, and Indy had just drafted Anthony Johnson and Ken Clark, who were both talented players. So this left me in a position of just taking up space, along with a few other rookies. We'd get into practices, but only sparingly, sometimes accidentally.

> **GRIFF NOTE:** *Be prepared to work hard.*

Nonetheless, I had come to camp ready to work.

Problem was, there wasn't much for me to do. I took part in only two plays during the preseason. I remember the running-back coach, Sylvester Crooms, who drafted me, telling me that I needed to be more physical. He didn't care for my style of play. I excelled at the goal-line plays, but because they already had a stacked backfield, I needed to show them something special if I was going to make the cut.

To make matters worse, the veterans gave the rookies a hard time from day one. They insisted that we sing our college fight songs at dinner—an old NFL tradition.

Give me a break.

They tried everything. But none of us were in the mood to mess around with those guys. I remember another rookie, a wide receiver from Chicago, spoke up one night. He looked one of the veterans dead in the eye and said, loud enough for the whole cafeteria to hear, "We won't be doing any singing."

It got real quiet in the lunchroom.

Then, they replied, "Well, we're going to come down to your room and wet all your stuff."

"Go ahead. Try it," the rookie said.

He challenged them. And you could tell from the expression on the guy's face that he was not joking around. He had had enough.

The veteran players continued to talk more stuff, but they never followed through.

I wasn't inter-
ested in anything
other than playing
ball, so all that other

GRIFF NOTE: *Keep your goal in sight at all times.*

"noise," I simply disregarded. I was paying attention to what was happening in practice and on game day. Because I wasn't getting any playing time, I knew the inevitable was about to happen.

When they started cutting people at the end of the preseason, they put notes on lockers. But when that day rolled around, I was already packed and in my car: "See you later." I was glad to be leaving.

I was released in the final cut.

The way I see it, if you're cut, you're cut. It doesn't matter whether it's the first cut or the last, the end result is the same—you're walking.

There was another guy on the team, one of the really big guys, whose name I don't remember. When they cut him, he shouted out, "Hoo-ha, now I can go to wrestling school!"

We were done with the Indianapolis Colts.

At the time, Indianapolis wasn't a very good team, so being cut wasn't the worst thing that could happen to you. The real question was:

What's the next move?

GRIFF NOTE: *Press on. Move forward.*

Days later, I got the call from Buffalo. I left immediately.

My buddy from Illinois, Henry Jones, was the Bills' first-round draft pick. So I was excited to be joining him. I started working out right away. I was scrimmaging against players who had been former first-round picks from earlier years, so I thought, "Hey, this is a great opportunity." I was impressed with Coach Marv Levy and the entire organization. Right after that workout, I was signed to the practice squad.

Now, being on a practice squad is like being an intern. You're doing all the grunt work, learning the ropes, and hoping that all of your work will result in a position on the team. Your whole game plan is about getting to the next level, landing the job. So I paid close attention to everything—on the field and off.

Buffalo was an interesting place.

The Bills had all the talent in the world, and they had been to the Super Bowl the year before, in 1990, but hadn't come home with the trophy. It was a real case study of team dynamics: What makes a talented team miss the mark? How does dissension between coaches and players play out on the field? What issues contribute to a talented team's inability to play well under pressure?

The Buffalo Bills were one of the most talented teams I'd ever played for.

I paid close attention to everything—on the field and off.

They had All-Pro players Bruce Smith, Thurman Thomas, Jim Kelly, Andre Reed, and Darrell Talley. All of them were at the top their game. *That* was the squad I was trying to make.

With all of that talent, I wondered if I'd ever get the chance to play. At the time, Buffalo's camps weren't competitive, in the sense that your playing meant you were vying for someone else's job. If you were a starter going into camp, you were a starter coming out; if you were a backup going in, you'd be a backup coming out, unless there was an injury. Also, the year before, the Bills had drafted fullback Carwell Gardner in the second round, though they didn't utilize the fullback in their no-huddle offense.

I had a bad feeling that I wasn't going to play. And worse than that, self-doubt kicked in, and I wondered:

Am I good enough to play in the NFL?

Up until that point, I had never wavered in my faith.

I was thoroughly frustrated. It's often a matter of timing, and it happens to the best of athletes. You have the ability and the tools, but you're simply in the wrong place at the wrong time. I think once you get to the pros, whether you are a free agent or a first-round draft pick, there simply isn't a great deal of opportunity to break through. It's a tough game to make a name for yourself.

"Am I good enough to play in the NFL?"

The challenges kept coming . . . but I overcame them, one by one.

GRIFF NOTES

Right before the game starts, right before that interview, right before your presentation…you're ready. You're confident because you've run through all of your drills. You know what you have to do, you understand what's expected of you. You may even be anxious or worried, which is natural. Your mental job is to keep a positive outlook regardless of what's happening around you. Go through possible scenarios in your mind, go through your drills, then realize at that point, there's nothing more you can do to prepare. It's time to show them what you've got.

At kick off, you're ready to roll.

•   **Accentuate the positive**.

Know your strong points and accentuate them on game day. When it's time to perform under pressure, use what you've got to get what you want.

•   **Don't lose sight of the goal**.

In most professional industries, including sports, rejection comes with the territory. When faced with opposition or rejection, keep your goal at the forefront. Consider the bigger picture. View each challenge as a necessary experience that will ultimately put you that much closer to your goal.

• **Be prepared to work hard.**

When called upon to contribute your part, be prepared to give it 100 percent. After all of the preparation, research, long hours, and hard work you've put in, game day is when it all pays off.

• **Press on. Move forward.**

The faster you can move beyond disappointments, the sooner you can get back on track and get down to the business of executing your game plan. Be aware of just how much time you spend mulling over your frustrations and disappointments, then work to cut that time in half.

5	1ST DOWN

AT BUFFALO, DILIGENCE WORKED IN MY FAVOR. Coaches looked at me and thought: "Howard is a hard worker. He knows his assignments."

Intangibles like character, integrity, personal commitment went a long way for me. Intangibles—important factors that don't show up on computers or grade sheets, that don't say if you are going to play fullback, you have to be this size, or if you're going to play tailback, you have to run this fast, but factors that contribute to the overall quality of a player.

Mentality has so much to do with the game.

> **GRIFF NOTE:** *Every part contributes to the whole.*

Take Buffalo, for instance. At that time, with all their talent, the Bills almost always seemed to fall short in the big games. One of the problems I noticed was the coaching staff's tendency to make certain players feel that the whole show relied solely on their individual performance. There were guys who were carrying the burden for the whole team, as opposed to the team working together as a unit to effect a win at the end of the day.

In my opinion, there was a feeling of dissatisfaction among many players with regard to the way the organization was run.

GRIFF NOTE: *Alienation causes dissension.*

The Bills had their star athletes …. every team does; however, the "stars" were the only players who were given any measure of respect, consideration, and responsibility. Preferential treatment alienated the rest of the team, which, I believe, had negative effects on game day. The lack of attention given to all aspects of the game resulted in continuous losses.

Although I had done well during the preseason at Buffalo, I was eventually cut. The coaching staff decided to keep only three backs active.

At that point, I was emotionally drained. I felt that I had done enough and simply couldn't handle another disappointment.

My football journey was over.

I had been hanging out with another buddy from Illinois, Darrick Brownlow, who had been signed by Buffalo during the off-season as a free agent. I told him, "I'm about to get out of here. I'm tired of all of this. I don't want to be bothered anymore. I'm going back to Chicago."

So I hopped in my car and was on my way home.

When I reached Cleveland, I called my girlfriend and checked in. She said the Bills had called. They wanted me back on the squad.

Replay

Huie Griffith,
Howard's father

I GOT A CALL FROM HOWARD'S FRIEND *Henry Jones, and he told me that Buffalo had put Howard on waivers, but they wanted to re-sign him. But they couldn't find him. Howard had packed up and left. I was very worried. And very upset. I started making all these phone calls all over the place. When Howard finally called, he told me, "I'm coming home."*

"No, you're not!" I said. "Don't show up at 9152 Clyde. Turn that car around—NOW."

He said, "No, I'm going to get a real job, use my degree."

"You've got a real job—with the Buffalo Bills."

He said, "I don't want to keep going through this. It's the same old thing. I'm still not going to be able to play. I'm not going to be able to make it because of their numbers. I'm tired of being embarrassed. They called me a living legend after scoring eight touchdowns against Southern Illinois, and now..."

"Go back and do what your coaches want you to do."

GRIFF NOTE: *Perseverance pays.*

My dad talked some sense into me, forcing me to turn the car around and go back. I was upset. I didn't care if the whole world was looking for me. The last thing I cared about was the Buffalo Bills and what they wanted. They couldn't make up their minds, so I'd do it for them. I didn't see the point of going back to get caught up in the same vicious circle. But I did what my father told me to do and headed back to Buffalo.

I didn't know where I fit in at Buffalo. I wasn't happy with what I saw, so once I got back, I started seeking other opportunities. I guess you could say I was covering my bases just in case they changed their minds about me a second time.

Though I continued to work hard, I was disheartened by the whole experience. This was not what I thought NFL ball would be. I expected a totally different atmosphere. Coming from Illinois, where respect, pride, and team spirit were high on the list of priorities, I could not believe what was happening up there. I wondered: Is it just Buffalo or the entire NFL?

Is this what I worked so hard for?

SIDELINE

Henry Jones
Defensive Back, Buffalo Bills

"I think that Howard was frustrated about not getting a fair opportunity to play in Buffalo. I don't think Howard was given an ample chance in preseason to show what he could do, and when you're put on the practice squad, you really are just waiting for someone to get hurt. No one did, so Howard couldn't show what he could do during the year. Plus, Buffalo had Thurman Thomas and Kenny Davis in a predominantly one back offense. They wanted Howard to play fullback where we had Carwell Gardner. I think Howard could have thrived in our one back offense given the opportunity. I think he felt that way, too."

SIDELINE

Dr. J. W. Smith, Former Head Football Coach
Percy L. Julian High School

"Howard had the misfortune of going to teams with one-back offenses. He was a tremendous halfback in college, but he didn't have the quick speed coaches look for out of a one-back. So, he was always behind someone. He never got the opportunity. It's tough when you can't see the light at the end of the tunnel. And he really didn't see the light in Buffalo. It was just one of those things."

At Buffalo, I witnessed, firsthand, how destructive self-centered behavior can be. There was not a feeling of camaraderie there at that time, and the team's performance in big games, namely Super Bowl games, told the whole story.

"Is this what I worked so hard for?"

I stayed on the practice squad for one year. But six weeks into my second year, I was released.

As soon as I was cut, San Diego picked me up.

I left the next day. And I left my car at my friend Henry's. I left my apartment "as is." I didn't even have time to pack my stuff. I just cut out of town. I was ready to move on.

It's funny because, just when you think you're at the end of your rope, another opportunity opens up and you're filled with hope again.

When I arrived in San Diego, the guys used to tease me because I wore shorts every day. They said, "People who live in California wear blue jeans. So we can always tell when people come from a cold place…they're in shorts twenty-four, seven."

Playing out the rest of the season in San Diego offered a different experience and gave me a better perspective on professional sports. I was beginning to see the importance of leadership. But don't get me wrong; San Diego wasn't any easier. In Indianapolis, I had to compete against Eric Dickerson and company; in Buffalo, there was Thurman Thomas; and in San Diego, it was Natrone Means, Ronnie Harmon, Marion Butts, and Rod Bernstein.

I had to continue proving myself.

I believe they call this a trend.

Each team that picked me up didn't necessarily need me. I had to continue proving myself.

But I made some advances. Coincidentally, the running-back coach at San Diego at that time was Sylvester Crooms, the same guy who had drafted me in Indianapolis. He saw me and said, "Man, you've changed!" Keep in mind this was a year and half later. As opposed to seeing a young, college body coming out, he was seeing a guy who had been working out year round. Physically, I had the look of an NFL player.

He told me I had developed into a good player, that it was like night and day compared to how I looked at Indianapolis. As I went through practice, he saw a lot of improvement. He was excited and glad to see that I had stuck it out.

Crooms wanted me to work hard on special teams because that was the way I was going to make the team. He was up front with me and kept me clued in to what was happening on the team. Ever since that time, we've stayed in contact with one another. We talk at least twice a year.

In 1992, I was in training camp with Marion Butts, who had a thigh bruise that kept him out the entire camp; and Rodney Harmon was holding out for a new contract. So that left Eric Bienemy, Natrone Means, and me. The head coach, Bobby Ross had a great work ethic and expected the best from his team. He had a certain way of doing things. He wanted each player to pay attention in practice and get in tune with the game plan.

We scrimmaged the Los Angeles Rams twice that year before playing them in a preseason game. Because I was an older player and had been around the game for a while, Coach Ross let me start the scrimmage in place of Natrone Means. They used me in short-yardage situations.

On my first carry I ran to the right side and got through, so I was one-on-one with my opponent. We were headed toward the sidelines, and I ran right through him. He ended up out of bounds, and I proceeded into the end zone. The Rams, unaware of the lineup

They found out later that I was "Howard something-or-other."

change, assumed I was Natrone Means. But in that particular scrimmage, only guys from the practice squad, as well as some of the rookies, were playing.

They found out later that I was "Howard something-or-other."

It was around this time that I caught the eye of the sports media and piqued the interests of other coaches in the league. My name was finally getting out there.

After that scrimmage game, the L.A. Rams took an interest in me. At the same time, I was also fine-tuning my blocking skills.

As a result of that game, I was placed in the goal-line package. And for the first time, I played fullback in all of the scrimmages. I played well throughout training camp; then one day Coach Crooms came up to me:

"I don't know what's going to happen, but we're going to try to keep you here. Thing is, it's out of my hands."

After training camp, the Los Angeles Rams went to the Chargers saying, "Hey, you can't keep this guy. You're not going to be able to keep him. We know what your numbers are."

So I continued to play well on special teams, doing everything I possibly could to ensure a spot on the team. Overall, I had a great preseason.

But the numbers game got the best of me at San Diego. Marion Butts had been hurt, and the Chargers had just drafted Natrone Means in the second round, who was obviously going to be their guy. They had a host of talented running backs. They had some first-round draft picks and some talented veterans. So they couldn't justify keeping me.

When it was time for cuts, who was going to get the axe? Marion Butts? Eric Bienemy, whom they had just drafted in the second round the year before? Of course not.

I was given my walking papers. Though I had made tremendous progress, there was just no room for me on the team. Why cut players who had produced for the organization? I was the sixth running back, and they only kept five. Once again, I was the odd man out.

My mom, Ruth Griffith, and me. (Griffith family collection)

That's me at nine years of age, ready for the big leagues. (Griffith family collection)

Kim and I went to my senior prom together back in '86. (Griffith family collection)

In action against Purdue during my sophomore season. (University of Illinois)

Breaking a couple of tackles, off I go again in my memorable game against Southern Illinois. (Mark Jones)

My Illini teammates carry me off the field after my NCAA record-breaking eighth touchdown vs. Southern Illinois. (Mark Jones)

Breaking a tackle in Illinois' 1989 victory over Ohio State. (Mark Jones)

Posing here with a cardboard cutout of the late, great Red Grange, whose touchdown record I broke in 1990. (Mark Jones)

The good old days, when I carried the ball for the Fighting Illini. (University of Illinois)

The world-champion Denver Broncos. (Full Field Panoramics)

The Mile High Salute follows Terrell Davis' touchdown
in Super Bowl XXXII. (*San Diego Union-Tribune*)

Meeting President Clinton after our first Super Bowl victory,
while Willie Green looks on. (The White House)

LAYING IT ON THE LINE

I was a member of the Los Angeles Rams from 1993 to 1994. (Gary Blumer)

I played for the Carolina Panthers from 1995 to 1996. (Robert Trevillian)

Me showcasing my talent when we played against Seattle. (Denver Broncos)

Kim and me after our wedding with friend/best man Darrick Brownlow and sister-in-law/maid of honor Karen Chilton. (Griffith family collection)

(Left to right) Will Smith, my high school coach; my wife Kim; me; and Dr. J.W. Smith, my high school head coach and mentor. (Griffith family collection)

Down in Arkansas, where they named the town after my family, I'm with my dad and my son, Howard II. (Griffith family collection)

Little Howard with his grandparents, Telia and Richard Chilton, in Miami for Super Bowl XXXIII. (Griffith family collection)

Joy and Huie Griffith with Little Howard in Miami for Super Bowl XXXIII. (Griffith family collection)

My stepmother, Joy, and me at the Super Bowl XXXIII victory party. (Griffith family collection)

The "Griffith Gang"—my wife, Kim, and our two sons, Howard II (left) and Houston (right). (Griffith family collection)

Coach Ross pulled me aside:

"Howard, there is nothing more you could have possibly done to make this team. It is truly a numbers game." He was sincere and well meaning. In my brief time on the team, I respected Coach Ross. He was a tough disciplinarian who expected all of his players to work as hard as they could. He also said, "I want to tell you something. Howard, you can play both positions—halfback and fullback. Start thinking about fullback."

Sylvester Crooms made the same suggestion. "Think about playing fullback," he said.

My mind reeled all the way back to my Mendel High School days. I was reliving the same conversation from all those years ago: "I want you to play fullback."

Only now there was much more at stake.

I considered the idea, knowing full well that it could keep me in the league. I gave it some thought: Fullback.

Fullback?

Fullback.

GRIFF NOTES

In the middle of the game, in the middle of the procedure, the first down is the equivalent of your first step. When you step up to the field, to the overhead projector, to the board of trustees, to the classroom full of students, it's time for you to go out and execute your game plan. It's the most important time for you. Now it's time to take everything you've learned all week and apply it.

In football, getting the first down is your first victory—you've moved the ball down the field. Continued first downs get you closer to the touchdown. But you've got to take the first step. What is your first down?

Maintaining an **EFFECTIVE TEAM** requires attention to not only the obvious talents of each player, but also the intangibles such as self-discipline, intelligence, knowledge of the game, and personal commitment.

A team leader should seek players who have a team consciousness, who aren't out to further their individual interests, but who bring their input and talents to the table for the good of the team.

Other ideas to consider:

- **Consider the intangibles.**

Character and integrity just can't be beat. A player's positive self-image, confidence, and disciplined attitude can actually save a team. These are the guys who help provide secondary leadership. They are motivators and leaders. It's important not to overlook the value of good character.

- **Every part contributes to the whole.**

No one player is more important than the sum total of a team effort.

- **Alienation causes dissension.**

Preferential treatment, or treating one player as more valued than another, can have damaging effects. Sure, some players' roles may be more demanding and may even require some extra attention, but alienating other players by overlooking their efforts can destroy team morale.

- **Perseverance pays.**

Keep it moving. Don't allow outside factors, or factors that are out of your control, to discourage you. Find ways around the "system." Again, you do that by revisiting your game plan. Why did you join this team? Why did you choose to play this particular game? What goals did you set out to accomplish? Trust that your hard work and dedication will result in a positive outcome, regardless of appearances.

6   THE OFFENSE

IN 1992, AFTER BEING RELEASED BY SAN DIEGO, the Los Angeles Rams sought me out. My position: I returned kickoffs for them and ... I played fullback.

From the start, I had the physical package to transform myself into a fullback, with a little bit of help from the weight room. I also had the ego-control and maturity to say, "Hey, look, this will keep you in the league. You're not going to carry the ball 25 times in a game and make a living. You're going to make your living blocking. Get used to it."

GRIFF NOTE: *Be realistic.*

Let's get this straight: Nobody wants to be a fullback.

Everybody wants to be a running back or a wide receiver, which is why there are dozens of running backs and receivers on the free-agent market every year. But fullback? Who wants to do the dirty work? I tease other players all the time by saying: "Listen, even when you are the top back, they're always looking for the next great talent to replace you." As much as they may want to replace the fullback, they can't. Fullbacks are so few and far between, mostly because nobody wants to play the position.

SIDELINE

Bucky Godbolt,
Former Illinois Running Back Coach

"I think the natural progression for him was to put that kind of weight on and be a fullback and block. He always knew how to block. Even when he played halfback, he was a blocker, and we spent a lot of time on that. All the guys I ever coached were very good blockers. They didn't have a choice because I remember when I was with John Mackovic, when you were a halfback, you had to block for the fullback and vice versa. You didn't have a choice. You weren't a battering ram. Everybody had to block."

I accepted the hard-hitting, no-hype, unglamorous, and often thankless position of an NFL fullback. Honestly, it is not an easy position to play. It's a tough game. We play a tough sport. But the thing is, not everyone in our sport is tough.

Not everybody wants to take on challenges.

If you can accept the fact that you're not going to the get the

ball anymore—which

is a difficult proposi-

tion—and understand

that becoming a great

> **GRIFF NOTE:** *Make adjustments.*

blocker is a viable position, then it gets easier. It requires a mental

and physical adjustment.

SIDELINE

Quintin Parker,
Former Illinois Strong Safety

"Man, I can honestly say, when I got to Illinois, Howard and I got on the field together, and he was backing me up, as a running back. My situation was that I was frustrated with the few opportunities I was given to play. And I wanted to get on the field, to be on the field at all times. So I moved to defense, to strong safety. Howard remained a running back, and next thing you know, he just grew. It's funny because I never, ever pictured Howard as a blocker. In fact, we used to tease him, "Hey, Howard, you're going to block somebody?" To see him now, you've got to respect him. He did what he had to do to play in the league, to be successful. Maybe the things he accomplished on the college level, he wasn't able to do on the professional level, but he found something he could do, and do well. So, it's just filled his whole game. He has a complete game now."

When I realized that I could be a difference-maker in a game, enabling my team to have a great rushing attack, I was able to reconcile the fact that my hard work might not ever show up in any headlines, in numbers, in stats. My performance would be reflected in the running back's stats.

GRIFF NOTE: *Recognize the possibilities.*

Mentally, I had to file away my memories of being a "star" running back at Illinois and relinquish my NFL dream of repeating in the pros what I had done in college.

The contrast was astounding.

Once, I had rushed for 263 yards in a single game at Illinois, and now, here I was with under 200 total rushing yards in my entire NFL career. I scored eight touchdowns in a victory over Southern Illinois, in which my 48-point performance broke Jim Brown's NCAA single-game scoring record of 43 against Colgate in 1956. Nonetheless, all of those accomplishments serve as a source of strength and a quiet reminder of what I was capable of, and of just how far I had come.

Becoming a fullback requires an understanding of leverage and positioning, knowing what guy you're blocking for and what his intentions are out on the field. So many guys just can't grasp it. They can't accept that fact that they are not going to be the marquis player. That's the primary reason there are only a handful of fullbacks in the league today who have become noteworthy. There are only five or six of us who can perform at a level that makes major differences in a game.

Working alongside players like Jerome Bettis and

Mentally, I had to file away my memories of being a "star" running back at Illinois.

Tim Lester, I was able to learn a great deal about blocking technique—leverage and getting lower than your opponent.

Chick Harris, the running-back coach, was very instrumental in helping me make the transition. In my first year with the Rams, I played primarily on special teams while studying the fullback position at the same time. I watched film and worked very closely with Tim Lester to gain a better understanding of the position.

The Rams were known for running the ball. In fact, the head coach, Chuck Knox, was nicknamed "Ground Chuck" because he loved to run the ball. We had a very young team. Most of us had only a few years' experience in the NFL. We had Chris Miller,

Todd Light, Shawn Gilbert—all very talented players. But we were young, and I think it showed in our performance.

And none of us could resist the L.A. nightlife.

"Man, you should have been at Roxbury's."

"Hey, did you check out Magic Johnson's party?"

There were so many distractions. I remember we used to hang out at former NBA player Norm Nixon's place called Creek Alley. It was a big hangout for celebrities and professional athletes.

The funny thing was that in L.A., the Rams were on the bottom rungs of celebrity status. We weren't always given carte blanche. Singers, actors, and other entertainers got the green light first, then us. But we didn't care; we wanted to party.

Although I became the Rams' starting fullback the next year, during the '93 season—which was a crucial step in my career—the team was going nowhere. I started 10 games that season, replacing Tim Lester.

Thinking back, had I stayed in L.A., I'm not sure I would have developed into the player I am today. It was difficult to concentrate in that city. The excitement was hard to ignore. There we were with money in our pockets, high-profile careers, and celebrities everywhere. All of us

GRIFF NOTE: *Prioritize.*

were young— talented, yes—but still with some serious growing up to do. There was no way we could deliver the way we should have out on the field. Our priorities weren't straight.

I remember Coach Harris used to talk to us about personal responsibility and how to handle ourselves off the field. He knew that the nightlife was a big distraction, so he would spend a great deal of time talking to us about upholding a certain image, watching our finances, staying focused—all of the things that could help us to become not just better players, but more responsible young men. Unfortunately, many of us failed to listen.

SIDELINE

Chick Harris,
Former L.A. Rams Running-Back Coach/
Carolina Panthers Running-Back Coach

"I think that sometimes young players go into the game thinking that the game, how fast they can run, or how good they are running the football, is the most important thing. But as I would have them in my meeting room, I could see some of the things that were taking place, some of the younger players were enjoying the social aspects of professional football and giving their jobs half the time needed in order for them to be top players. So I tried to make them realize that their responsibility was not just about the new clothes they could buy or the new cars they could buy, but also to go out and take care of family, and present an image of a professional . . . and exemplify leadership, no matter how hard the job was, no matter how hard the instruction for the day, you've got to survive it."

Personally, I felt that playing for the L.A. Rams was a necessary step in my growth as a fullback. It was an opportunity to play in the NFL and, at the same time, learn all I could about the position that would eventually become *my* position. It was my chance to learn what winning was all about and the importance of focus, study, and concentration.

After a fairly disappointing season, the Rams decided against using a fullback in the traditional sense, so I was placed in the expansion draft. The Carolina Panthers and the Jacksonville Jaguars were looking for a few good men.

GRIFF NOTES

When I changed positions and became a fullback, I developed a whole new appreciation for what it meant to play on offense. It opened my eyes to all of the elements that go into having a solid running game. I welcomed the challenge. A new position or a new role on a team doesn't have to be an insurmountable task. But it does require that you understand, study, and familiarize yourself with every aspect of that new position, learning how that new role will affect the team overall.

- **Be realistic.**

  Approach your new position openly, but with realistic expectations. Grow into it.

- **Recognize the possibilities.**

  Motivate yourself by examining the potential that the new position offers.

- **Make adjustments.**

Adjust your routine, structural goals, and personal game plan according to the requisites of your new position.

- **Prioritize.**

Putting things in their proper perspective and prioritizing is an ongoing job. You should always continue to take inventory, reassess your situation, and make necessary adjustments. It's the best way to stay on top of your game.

7   THE DEFENSE

MY CAREER JUMP-STARTED when I was selected by the Carolina Panthers in the 1995 Expansion draft. I was happy about the opportunity to play for a new team where I could make a name for myself. By that time, I had gotten myself in top physical and mental condition, and I actually had begun to enjoy playing fullback.

Coincidentally, Coach Chick Harris had joined the Panthers organization as well. So I had him as a support system to assist me further in developing my style of play as a fullback.

However, in spite of all the great potential a new team offered, playing on an expansion team has its share of pitfalls.

Our first year was horrible.

Everything that could have gone wrong *went* wrong.

We were all in a funk by the end of the season.

Then, the '96 season unfolded like a Hollywood script. Carolina devised a blocking scheme, and I was the main ingredient. That year, we averaged 96.5 rushing yards in the first four games of the season, and that number later increased to 148. Eventually half-back Anthony Johnson turned in consecutive 100-yard performances.

We became the NFL's seventh-best rushing team.

Our running game in Charlotte was simple but over-powering. I'd knock out the linebacker,

GRIFF NOTE: *Analyze your game.*

and Anthony Johnson would follow on my heels. If you want to know what it feels like to be a blocking back, you can stand in front of a garage door about ten yards away and continue to ram into the door about 25 times. That's what it's like to play this position. So I kept slamming into the "garage door" and eventually, it gave way. Defensive tackle Mark Dennis once described it by saying, "It's like having an offensive guard in the backfield."

My teammates noticed my determination to be a difference-maker as fullback. I had begun to analyze the game in ways that I had never done before.

SIDELINE

Kerry Collins,
Former Quarterback, Carolina Panthers

"I can see his neck getting shorter and shorter as the game goes on. Howard is like a human battering ram out there, really. Those linebackers are coming hard. He's done a great job at it. He's gone up there with reckless abandon and taken those guys on. He's the guy who makes the play go."

SIDELINE

Matt Elliot,
Former Offensive Guard, Carolina Panthers

"Howard is legitimately the unsung hero."

SIDELINE

Chick Harris,
Running-Back Coach, Carolina Panthers

"When we were looking at the draft board, looking for who we could pick at fullback, I thought Howard would be the guy. And I was very lucky to be able to get him. Howard came into a situation where another coach had brought his player from Chicago, who was a very good player, Bobby Christian, and we were battling on who was the better player. And sometimes things didn't always seem like they were fair, and Howard became frustrated. But I told him: 'The only thing you can do is your best, and let things lay the way they're going to lay.' And sure enough, he continued to work, continued to do the hard grunt work, and it played out at the end, where he was the starter and was executing plays.

"He was a leader, no question about it. There are different types of leaders. Howard exemplified a work ethic, a determination that was second to none on our football team. And you could see players start to gravitate toward him. He was about getting the job done. He would take time out with young players and talk about plays and scrimmages that were difficult. He was similar to the squad captain in a combat situation. It was like "Saving Private Ryan," you could say. All of a sudden you have a guy, there are a lot of bullets flying, there are a lot of obstacles, but he was one of the guys who could forge ahead."

I appreciated the nod. I was working harder than ever, especially physically. My body was not used to taking that kind of beating, so I had to bulk up.

And our philosophy was: Be physical.

Kevin Greene set the tone.

Greene's intensity is unmatched, especially during the countdown to a game. Bill Romanowski pales in comparison, which is saying something because Romo's intensity is a sight to see. Greene didn't toss chairs or punch walls, but his war cries bounced off the walls of the locker room. Coach Capers would be in the middle of his pregame speech, but he could hardly be heard because of all the noise Greene was making.

Be physical.

The only way to earn respect in this game is to be physical against your opponent.

I developed my football mentality at Carolina. I learned a lot from Kevin Greene, who made a persuasive case for hard-nosed toughness, which I now incorporate into my game. That season, the quarterback, Kerry Collins, was riding high because we were running the ball. If it was third-and-four, we could throw the slant pass to Willie Green, who had the ability to convert it to

> *The only way to earn respect in this game is to be physical with your opponent.*

a big gainer. Or throw the big strike to Wesley Walls and Mark Carrier.

But Carolina was a difficult place for Kerry Collins. It definitely didn't help that he liked to drink, not in a town like Charlotte. Keep in mind, we were in the Bible Belt. We had an image to uphold, an image that Kerry compromised by his behavior off the field. It was probably the worst possible city for him to be in. If he had been drafted by a different organization, those issues would never have come up. He was clearly uncomfortable.

Despite his personal problems, Kerry led our team to some terrific highs. We were playing solid ball and taking the league by storm. No one expected an expansion team to do so well, so quickly. Things were definitely on the upswing.

MY SON, HOWARD GRIFFITH II, was born on September 21, 1996, right before an away game in San Francisco. After I returned to Carolina, and during the next home game the following week, his name was up in lights on the scoreboard announcing his arrival.

A couple of months later, I played in front of my son for the first time. He was only 10 weeks old.

My wife, Kim, and Howard II were back at the apartment. They weren't going to the game that day because of the bad weather. But Carolina's owner, Jerry Richardson, approached me in the chapel before the game. He said, "I'm going to call and see if they want to come to the game. Let me put them in a suite." So they were able to see the game live, from inside the box. This gesture on Richardson's part added to my feeling that Carolina was a classy organization. I always felt very much at home there.

SIDELINE

Kim Griffith,
Howard's wife

"We were so excited. I was jumping up and down with the baby in one arm, and cheering with the other one. Up until that day, I had never been present when Howard scored a touchdown in his pro career, but for some reason I had a feeling that he would that day. It was a special time for us."

After the game, I remember standing in the end zone, looking up at the luxury box, and at that moment, everything in my life was put in its proper perspective. It was the first time I'd played in front of my son. I even scored a touch-

GRIFF NOTE: *Keep the proper perspective.*

down that day with 8:02 left in the third quarter. We won that game, 24-0, over Tampa Bay.

I know my son won't remember seeing my touchdown that day, although Kim said that he stayed awake through the whole game. But he will have to hear about that game in the years to come, and it's bound to grow in importance over the years. I haven't decided how I'm going to tell him about it. But I do know, while it might have been a one-yard run back then, by the time I start telling him the story, it will be five yards or six yards, and before you know it, it'll be 99 yards.

Everything changed after Howard was born. The account-ability factor is so dif-

I believe things happen for a reason.

ferent when you have a family. Suddenly, it wasn't about me any-more. Howard II became the focus. Before he came along, I don't know if I could say that I'd die for someone else. Now, I can.

The headline in *The Charlotte Observer* read: "LITTLE GRIFF BRINGS NEW LIFE TO HIS FATHER."

At the time, Kim and I weren't married. We had been plan-ning our wedding for about a year when Kim found out she was pregnant. Some people wanted us to get married immediately, be-fore the baby was born, but we had already set our date, April 19, my Dad's 70 birthday. And we were determined to get married on our terms.

I believe things happen for a reason.

We had been dating since high school. We even went to prom together! So, of course, we had a tight bond. We were ready. The way we saw it, little Howard was a pre-wedding gift.

That season, the Panthers made it to the playoffs. In our NFC playoff game against Dallas, I realized something that actually surprised me: the Cowboys' linebackers were intimidated by me.

I had a reputation and didn't even know it.

We had routinely run the same play, off the right side, four consecutive times. They knew it was coming, but they couldn't do anything to stop it. They certainly tried, but their instincts betrayed them. If I made it past the line of scrimmage, the linebacker had to make a decision—take me on, or avoid me. If he tried to run around me, the hole would grow bigger.

A good running game breaks a defense's will. And that day, we broke the will of the Cowboys.

It was a big win for us. In fact, every win that season made everyone hopeful that we'd break out of the typical mold of expansion teams, that we'd become the expansion team that broke through all the barriers.

After the victory, we were whooping it up in the locker room, when Willie Green said, "We need to go back outside and thank our fans because if it wasn't for them, we wouldn't be here." So the whole team ran back onto the field, and we applauded our fans. They went crazy. And for all of the players, it was an unforgettable moment.

I was riding high.

No one expected Carolina to make it to the championship game. They all thought it would be Dallas vs. Green Bay, but the Carolina Panthers shocked the world. We played in the NFC championship game the following week.

It was great to be playing for the NFC title. But the mystique of the Green Bay Packers got the best of us. We prepared for that game, but when it was time to come out and play, we faltered. Though there was a lot of highlight footage of my touchdown reception—the only touchdown of the game—it didn't do much for my disposition. I was deeply disappointed by that loss.

Although we lost the NFC title game, I felt good about my overall accomplishments at Carolina. Things had come together. Kim and I were preparing to build a house in Charlotte. The Panthers were on the move. We had a beautiful baby boy. I was a free agent, primed and ready for the big payoff with the Panthers.

But the Panthers had other plans.

They were obsessed with the San Francisco 49ers system, the West Coast passing game, which meant they considered a blocking fullback expendable. The organization was $2 million dollars under the cap, maybe more. Carolina could have signed me with the money and still gone out and signed anyone it wanted, but in the end, they choose not to.

It was a business move. Pure and simple. Despite all of the successes, the great performances, and the victories, the Carolina Panthers decided not to re-sign me.

It was a big blow.

But what do you do?

You call your agent and go job hunting.

GRIFF NOTES

Three words describe the great strides we made at Carolina:

- **Effort**
- **Energy**
- **Execution**

As a team, we put our heart and soul into making that team a viable member of the NFL. We learned a lot along the way, all of which served to fuel our continued efforts in the league. A new team, a new organization always provides a learning ground. You make the best of the opportunity, and you take from it only the good.

Individually, I was able to fine-tune my skills as a fullback. I learned to analyze the game in real specific detail. The huge disappointment I experienced at the end of my two years forced me to look at my life and career and put things in their proper perspective. I had nothing to complain about...the future was brighter than ever.

8 SPECIAL TEAMS

MY FIRST FREE-AGENCY TRIP WAS TO DENVER.

In 1997, I met Bobby Turner, the Broncos' running-back coach. He wanted me to be Terrell Davis' blocking back. We went out to breakfast together, and we talked football through the entire meal. After we had been in the restaurant over an hour, Turner turned to the waitress and placed another order for the same meal he had just had. He piled up all these pancakes and eggs and continued talking football.

After his second meal was done, he said: "Hey, man, we want you here. I've got you as the No. 1 fullback available. I told Mike [Shanahan] that you could help us get to the next level."

Bobby Turner is a talented coach, and at the time, he was part of an organization that was hungry for a Super Bowl win. The Jacksonville defeat from the prior season was still haunting the Broncos, and they believed I could make a difference. Coach Turner lobbied to head coach Shanahan to sign me.

That same day, I received the word from Coach Shanahan: "You're not leaving town until you sign with us." I was scheduled to make a trip to Detroit and a few other cities, but they wanted a commitment right then and there. They didn't want me to leave until I had signed on the dotted line. And they promised to make it worth my while.

SIDELINE

Huie Griffith,
Howard's father

"I get this call from him, and he's saying that he's made up his mind. Made up his mind? He's supposed to visit three, four more teams, and he's made up his mind? Whoa, wait a minute. I said, 'Start giving me some reasons.' 'Well,' he said, 'they're not hassling me about getting money. And they've got a chance to win the Super Bowl. They told me I'm the missing link to get them where they want to go.' So I could tell he was very serious."

I called home and said, "I'm a Denver Bronco." I had joined Mike Shanahan, Terrell Davis, and John Elway.

SIDELINE

Kim Griffith,
Howard's wife

"When I received the phone call from Howard, I knew that he should have been en route to Detroit. So, naturally, the first thing I asked him was 'Where are you?' And his response was Denver. 'Well, what are you still doing there?' 'I'm a Denver Bronco,' he said. I'm thinking, 'Denver Bronco? What is he talking about?' So I started thinking: He hasn't gone to Detroit yet, so how could he be a Denver Bronco? He's supposed to be in Detroit with Barry Sanders. Blocking for Barry Sanders. People will really recognize his talent then—not to mention it's close to home, Chicago. We can't go to Denver in the cold and snow.

"But as I listened to Howard tell me the terms of his Denver deal, I realized that he had clearly made the right decision. And it has proven to be the best, most timely decision he could have ever made. So, here we are in Denver...and it's not so cold after all."

GRIFF NOTE: *Credit secondary leadership.*

I was excited, but there was no time to celebrate. Coach Turner had to get me ready to play. Everyone should know that African-American coaches, particularly assistants, have a difficult time moving up in the system. And running-back coaches rarely get their due. It's assumed to be an easy position to coach—"Just let 'em run." That's the attitude. Take Terrell Davis—he was a sixth-round pick. He is a tremendous talent, but someone had to bring it out of him. Someone had to prime the well. Of course, Coach Shanahan and Terrell's teammates helped, but much of the credit should go to Bobby Turner. He deals with Terrell one-on-one, day after day.

> **GRIFF NOTE:** *Be able to prepare while under fire.*

Now, he had me to deal with.

Bobby had to make sure that I played like he said I could play. His reputation was on the line. And so was mine. We were both under pressure.

We had to hit the pavement running.

SIDELINE

Randall Townsel,
Friend/Former Julian Football Player

"When Howard told me he was going to play for the Denver Broncos, I thought: He'll finally get the attention his talent deserves. We gave him a send-off party before he left for Denver. And I remember talking to him, and one of the things I said was that Denver was a highly visible team where people would be able to really see his ability. You don't go from running eight touchdowns in one game, being a Big Ten tailback, to just being able to block. His entire career, Howard scored big touchdowns and made big plays. So I really expected Shanahan to utilize him in the offense. I thought Howard would be in the position to catch 40 or 50 balls a year...and so did he."

Under Coach Turner, I was able to perfect my blocking ability. He has this saying: "The low man wins." That's what blocking is all about.

If Terrell came in and rushed for 900 yards that year, they were going to come after me. I would be the first man in the line of fire. I had to prove that I deserved every penny of my new contract.

I had to prove that I deserved to replace Aaron Craver, the fullback they released to take me on.

Now, everybody liked Craver, especially Terrell. And Terrell's opinion mattered most.

So there was no margin for error.

At camp, before our first preseason game, I hurt my thumb while blocking Bill Romanowski. I tried to conceal it, but you could see the bone. I didn't leave the practice. I didn't let up. I wanted to show my teammates how committed I was to the team. Finally, Reggie Rivers, a former player who is now a sports broadcaster, had to tell me, "Call it a day, Howard. Get some help."

SIDELINE

Terrell Davis,
Tailback, Denver Broncos

"It looked bad. If it had been me, it would have sidelined me for a while. But instead, he just had the thumb taped up, put a brace on it, and went on. When you talk to a player, you can get a sense of what he's like. After practicing with Howard a few times, and the way he was working on the field, I could tell a lot about him. He'd get upset when he'd make mistakes—small mistakes. I knew at that time he was dedicated to being the very best. We clicked from day one. It took us a little time to get that tight bond, but once it got going, we were a perfect match.

"Our No. 1 asset is how well we work together. Not only on the field but off. It's almost like if you have brotherly love for someone, you don't want that person to get hurt. So you're going to do anything you can to protect that person. We're really cool off the field. We can talk about what's going on, knowing the game. That process got started at training camp. After that San Francisco game, I thought of the line from *Casablanca*. It's true: That was the start of a great relationship."

I realized the difference between being hurt and being injured. There are times when you have to suck it up, go out, and get the job done because there are people counting on you. There are other instances when you call in the team physician.

I didn't suit up in Mexico City for our first exhibition game. I watched from the sidelines, and I saw the team collapse right in front of my eyes. At least it appeared that way when John Elway came to the sideline with a shoulder injury. One look at his injury and you would have thought, "He's finished."

Ten days later, we all stood by at our training camp field in Greeley, nervously waiting to see how Elway would perform. Well, he threw the ball better than ever. In fact, he insisted that his arm felt stronger than it had before the injury. I'd heard all the stories about Elway's arm. In training camp, I was impressed. But I didn't realize how strong it actually was until the season began. During warm-ups, he threw a pass that reached me before I'd even realized it was on its way.

That's John Elway.

I also sat out a preseason game against my former teammates at Carolina. By the final preseason game, I was back in action.

Terrell went berserk against San Francisco in that final exhibition game. They didn't know what hit them. We both had a lot of fun. Terrell said, "You know what? This is the beginning of a great relationship."

That was a big turning point for us. Even though he was close to Aaron Craver, I knew he fully supported me. I had made my mark.

GRIFF NOTE: *Join forces.*

Looking back, it took every ounce of strength for me to survive what I now call my NFL "apprenticeship." When I think of all the teams that cut me, I wonder how I ever made it through. At any point between Indianapolis and Carolina, I could have quit. And just when I thought I had found a place to hang my hat, in Carolina, even that eluded me.

A professional life in the NFL is a gamble. You take your chances. And it is very fleeting. But along the way, you must evaluate just how much it means to you to keep going. There are certainly enough roadblocks to discourage you every few steps. But is it worth it? You're constantly asking yourself that question.

Denver was the deal. And timing made all the difference. The Broncos needed me and I needed them.

Playing for the Broncos, I realized that mental preparation was

GRIFF NOTE: *Go the extra mile.*

going to make all the difference in my game. So I created a rigorous schedule for myself, a time to work out, a time to study, and a time to review film. I became part of the breakfast club, getting to the facility in the early hours of the morning. I made a habit of working out before everyone got there, before our meetings started.

When it's time to go over plays for the upcoming game, it's like I'm back in college again. I'm taking notes with the best of them. I'm writing down plays—the name of the play and what my responsibility is as it pertains to the play. I highlight my assignments as we go through the playbook. Then, I prepare as much as I can for improvisation out on the field. If you have a handle on the general game plan, you're always ready for an audible call.

Coach Shanahan's methods are sound and sure. He has a knack for going in and studying his opponents, not only during the week we're playing them, but in the weeks leading up to that game. We will do something in a game one Sunday that has an effect on our games down the road. So our opponents don't ever have a clear-cut idea of what to expect. They'll have so much film to watch that they can't possibly hone in on our game plan on any given Sunday.

Coach Shanahan believes that everything starts with coaching. And he allows his coaches to coach. He expects the coaches to convey the game plan, clearly and thoroughly, to the players. His confidence in his assistant coaches allows him the freedom he needs to spend the day thinking about a game two weeks ahead of time.

Shanahan's always thinking ahead.

He gives out a lot of information each week, adjusting

GRIFF NOTE: *Devise strategies that stretch.*

our strategy, so that from week to week, we are somewhat unpredictable. Sure, we have tendencies. We may run the ball to the left a lot, but opponents are going to see so many different formations that they don't know where the ball is going.

Coach Shanahan challenges us to learn different formations and different blocking schemes week in and week out. And it helps the players because, this way, you don't get caught in a comfort zone where you think, "Well, we're going to make this play this week, and this is what we'll do for the entire 16 weeks."

The way I see it: If you want to be a champion, you use the formula. You follow the game plan. And you learn the technique of improvisation.

> *The way I see it: If you want to be a champion, you use the formula.*

Our routines stay the same as far as our weekly schedule and curfew are concerned, but the information we get from our meetings can change daily. And when Wednesday comes and we have our group meeting, so much is coming at you that you've got to stay on your toes. Come Sunday, no one's interested in any excuses.

Coach Shanahan expects every player to adopt a winning attitude, and understand that a heavy workload is what's required of champions.

During training camp, he plans a lot of outside activities for the guys to help break the monotony. Days before camp, he has a fishing derby, and right after camp, he has a big party at his home where he invites not only the team, but the wives and kids, too. People outside of the league may not understand just how generous that is, and what a huge difference it makes in team morale. The NFL lifestyle isn't easy on our families. They have to live in cities where they have no friends or relatives, where their husbands are gone half the time, practicing, traveling, or playing. Shanahan understands that if your wife's not happy at home, if your kids are bored and tired of being cooped up in the house, more than likely, you're going to have hear about it, and you can't help but bring that to the workplace.

The Denver Broncos are a special team. We shoot for perfection.

So he's always looking for an edge. Anything he can do to make the team more comfortable, more of a cohesive unit, increase morale and make team players out of us all, he does it.

The Denver Broncos are a special team. We shoot for perfection.

GRIFF NOTES

SPECIAL TEAMS:

Here's your backup. These are teammates who go in and do the hard work that they don't necessarily get credit for. For example, in a corporate environment, there are the front men, the leaders or top executives. But they're supported by a lot of "special-teams" players who get the grunt work done. After you've delivered your offensive scheme, you bring in your special-teams players and allow them to clarify specific areas of your game plan.

On the football field, the special teams are so important because they determine where we're going to get the ball, from an offensive standpoint. And from a defensive standpoint, they determine how far they can pin the opposing offense in its own territory. All of this is just another aspect of getting the job done.

POINTS OF INTEREST:

- **Credit secondary leadership.**

Although there's only one team leader, there are many secondary leaders who assist in a team's effectiveness. The importance of their role must be acknowledged and respected. In football, it could be an assistant coach on offense or defense; in a corporate situation, it may be middle management or the administrative staff. Whatever the team environment, secondary leadership plays an important part in the execution of the game plan.

• **Prepare while under fire.**

When on a tight deadline, you are most effective if you create a strict routine for yourself, prioritize daily and weekly goals, and focus most of your energy into the immediate business at hand.

• **Join forces.**

When you're in a shared role on a team, meaning a role in which you provide direct support for another player, join forces and create ways in which your "double-teaming" can best be utilized.

• **Go the extra mile.**

When the stakes are high, increased discipline and hard work are in order. Going the extra mile may mean putting in extra research time, extra training, extra work on a specific project. If you pace yourself, the extra work will bring positive end results.

- **Devise strategies that stretch.**

When creating strategies for specific projects, design them in such a way that leaves room for adjustments. Always be prepared to improvise.

9 THE BLOCK

SOON AFTER I SIGNED WITH DENVER, I ran into my old coach from Carolina, Dom Capers. "You're going to be playing for a great coach," he told me. "He has control over everything in his organization." Clearly, it was a difficult time for Capers. After putting all the pieces together at Carolina and leading the Panthers to the NFC championship, he wasn't able to keep his team intact.

But there was a power struggle between general manager Bill Polian and the owner, Jerry Richardson, which caused conflict within the organization. I remember Richardson saying on one occasion: "This is my organization." He has two sons—one of them is now the president, and the other is in charge of stadium operations. So he had people in place who he trusted, which is why he wasn't willing to turn his team and his business over to Bill Polian.

Eventually, the franchise self-destructed. Did it have to go down like that? Of course not.

When the Panthers came to Mile High, we beat them, and I could see that the wheels were coming off the Panthers. The unraveling began in a preseason game, when Bill Romanowski nearly beheaded Kerry Collins.

When Romo broke Kerry's jaw, he broke his will right along with it. And it was down hill from that point on for the Panthers.

We opened the regular season with a home game against Kansas City. Although we won, 19-3, I didn't play well—at least not by my standards. Naturally, I wanted my first game to be a huge success. "It's a learning process," Coach Turner reminded me.

The next game belonged to Ed McCaffrey.

He caught three touchdown passes on Seattle's rookie cornerback, Shawn Springs. Springs didn't respect Ed as a receiver. A big mistake. I don't know how fast Ed is on the clock. But I do know that when he gets the ball in his hands, he gets where he's going. So Ed sees a rookie, Shawn Springs, across the line of scrimmage, and he's getting no respect. Big mistake. When you run your mouth and you don't know your opponent, you're buying into the hype. All Shawn Springs had to do was study the film to know that he should not have underestimated Ed McCaffrey's ability.

Underestimation only makes you more vulnerable. You must respect every team's talent and ability to play the game; otherwise, you leave yourself open to mistakes and miscalculation.

A couple of weeks later, we beat the Bengals, 38-20, and Terrell ran for more than 200 yards for the first time in his career.

At that point, a Denver newspaper story pointed out that Davis was on track for a 2,000-yard season. He was averaging 131.5 yards per game. He needed to average 123 yards in the remaining 12 games to step into history alongside O. J. Simpson and Eric Dickerson. And that's when everyone became obsessed with his yardage, and the microscope zoomed in. Week after week, the world kept score.

I had been a running back, so I could think like Terrell. And he'd been a fullback, so he could think like me.

Underestimation only makes you more vulnerable.

Our run ended in Atlanta when I was blocking for Terrell, and he cut it all the way to the backside and got tackled dead in my knee. I was devastated.

Why now?

Coach Shanahan came back to me on the flight home and said, "Don't worry about it. We'll be all right. Get your four or five weeks and you'll come back ready to play."

Five weeks?

I told him I'd be ready for the next game—a Monday night game against New England.

The pain was excruciating. I had to have the fluid drained from my knee twice a week. I wanted to play. I needed to play. I worried all the time about not holding up my end, after they'd given me the big money. This was an opportunity to show my teammates how important it was for me to play.

I had a simple rationale for the whole thing. The injury may have held me back as far as running was concerned, but I don't run the ball much anyway. And they throw to me only occasionally, so I thought, even though I wasn't 100 percent, I could still block.

When Terrell walked into the locker room on Monday and saw me getting ready to play, he said, "Are you crazy?"

"I've got my brace," I said, "Let's go."

SIDELINE

Detron Smith,

Fullback/Special-Teams Ace, Denver Broncos

"He's mentally strong. That's something I respect a lot. I've seen him in pain and he's still steady going. A lot of guys

> would say, 'Come in for a minute and relieve me.' It was no surprise whatsoever when he played Monday, because that's the type of mentality he has. Even though he's not 100 percent or even 85 percent, Howard's still going to go out and try to play. You can't ask more than that out of a player."

Terrell rushed for 171 yards that night. Afterward, New England safety Willie Clay made an observation: "Davis is the man. In order to beat the Broncos, you've got to stop Terrell Davis. John Elway is a Hall of Fame quarterback and all, but a championship team has a good running game. And they've got a helluva running game."

In fact, we'd just rolled over them. New England linebacker Todd Collins went as far as saying:

"You don't need Elway when you have Davis. We couldn't stop them. There wasn't anything magical. It was just a good old butt kicking."

So it was "Terrell Time."

The sports media began reporting on the "awesome Denver offense," and our running game. We were the focus. And I must say, it felt good to be recognized as having one of the best offenses in the league. The "Mile High salute" that the backs initiated became a regular fixture in every game. They started calling Mike Shanahan, "Mike The Mastermind." And a spot was being warmed for Elway in the Hall of Fame.

The hype had begun. And it only got bigger as the season progressed.

I had never played in Oakland. I'd never seen all of the mystique and black-and-silver stuff up close. It was something to see. The fans are remarkably hyped in Oakland. The energy in that stadium is incredible. Fans are so pumped up that if you're not prepared for it, it can be a huge distraction.

Oakland turned out to be our worst nightmare. Napoleon Kauffman was in rare form. That day, he could score from anywhere on the field and make everyone miss. But we didn't take care of business on the defensive end. It's a team game, and all three units have to be on the same page for the duration. And that day, it was like we had all read different playbooks. We were scrambling.

The hype had begun. And it only got bigger as the season progressed.

In every game, if one unit is off, the other two must dominate. And that day, the other two faltered.

It was a terrible loss.

You can't cakewalk through a season. On the other hand, you can't gloss over defeats. When we lose, we study film with our coach, who's more critical than ever. Your first impulse is to tune it out because who wants to hear negative things about his performance? But it's important to pinpoint your errors, even if it momentarily hurts your pride.

This is what makes Shanahan a great coach. Nobody is exempt from criticism. His standards are so high. Shanahan's view is this: We need to know what the problem is. If you can't take care of business, then let us know; we'll get somebody else in there who can. He always seeks out the weak link and looks for ways to strengthen the team.

And trust me, you don't want to be the weak link.

> *It's important to pinpoint your errors, even if it momentarily hurts your pride.*

The accountability factor is extremely high. No one wants to be the reason a play didn't work.

After nine games, Terrell Davis was averaging 100 yards per game. There were only two times that he was under 100. Both of those times, I was on the sideline. So the buzz began. Backup tailback Vaughn Hebron said, "Howard's the best run blocker in the business." Then Shannon Sharpe said, "Look at Terrell's numbers, he's usually following Howard Griffith." My stock started to rise when the work I was doing was seen as having a direct effect on Terrell's game.

Headlines

"Bronco's Griffith Noticed by His Absence" Reprinted from Nando.Net/Newsroom 10/11/97 by Alex Marvez (Scripps Howard News Service):

"Howard Griffith is rarely noticed until he's gone. When Griffith, the Denver Broncos' starting fullback, wasn't on the field on Sept. 28 against Atlanta, tailback Terrell Davis failed to reach 100 yards rushing for the only time this season. When Griffith returned for Monday's game against New England, Davis rushed for 171 yards in a 34-13 victory.

"Carolina tailback Anthony Johnson rushed for 1120 yards with five 100-yard games. After six games [the following] season, Johnson finds himself on pace for 765 yards and has mustered only one 100-yard performance.

"Coincidence? Hardly.

"Griffith doesn't expect to garner the spotlight for his work as a blocker. That's just the nature of playing fullback. Davis, though, is definitely appreciative. With Griffith paving the way, Davis has compiled a 52-yard rushing average and is on pace for a 2,069-yard season. Denver (6-0) also will be the NFL's only undefeated team entering its next game, Oct. 19 at Oakland."

Positive reinforcement from my teammates is always a big boost for me. The press I was getting was also reassuring. I was finally satisfied that I was getting the job done.

SIDELINE

Terrell Davis,
Tailback, Denver Broncos

"Griff is the piece of the puzzle that we need—a dependable fullback. We tend to run the ball a little bit more when Griff's back there. I think the attitude is different. A lot fullbacks don't get the credit. I mean, you've got 'Moose' [retired Dallas fullback Daryl Johnston], who blocks for Emmitt [Smith], but that's sort of been established throughout the years. Howard doesn't get the credit he deserves, but that seems like the unsung hero position on most football teams."

The way I see it, I have the ultimate blue-collar job in football. Even the linemen get tired of blocking. And when I'm pass blocking, the defensive linemen get a running start at you. On a run, you're trying to meet the guy on the other side of the line of scrimmage. When you meet up with him, you're in an all-out war.

And I don't like to lose any plays.

I don't like to be seen on film losing on a play. Now, I know I'm not going to win 100 percent of the time, but Terrell believes that I am. So do my teammates. I go into games wanting to dominate. So does my opponent. But I go in with the mind-set that I have to dominate in order for us to be successful. So I do whatever it takes.

GRIFF NOTE: *Give it all you've got.*

No matter what the conditions.

SIDELINE

Terrell Davis,
Tailback, Denver Broncos

"A fullback has to know where the halfback is going. He has to have the instincts and know that the play is designed to go in, but also where I would go if I was the runner. Howard does a great job doing that for me. His guy could be on the outside, yet there's a huge hole in the inside; therefore he knows where I'm going. If he was the runner, he'd go there, too, and so now he's going to lead me to the hole. Not every fullback does that. Some go where they're taught to go. They go by rote.

"On film, you can see how other fullbacks play. That's when you really appreciate how valuable Howard Griffith is. It's instinctive with him. Howard makes adjustments on the run because he is such a good runner himself.

"I can tell what's he doing by just looking at him. I don't have to say anything. We don't have to talk. I know what he's thinking by the way he's looking at me. I mean, a lot of times I can't hear him in split-back formation and he can't hear me. We have hand signals for different things, just to make sure we're on the same page. I don't know who else does it; I don't know if it's rare or not, but when I watch film, I see us doing things on film that I don't see other backs doing. As soon as we get in a stance, we always look at each other. That's the one thing we do. We have to make sure we're on the same page."

Buffalo vs. Denver—the biggest October snowstorm in recent years hit Denver.

How in the world are we going to get to Buffalo?

My wife got up about 4 a.m. because little Howard was still waking up in the middle of the night at that time. She took one look outside and said, "Howard, I don't think you're going to be playing in Buffalo on Sunday." I looked out and thought the same thing.

What was I thinking?

All the money had been spent, all the commercials sold. The NFL told us: "Go to Buffalo."

"They can't be serious," my wife said.

They were dead serious.

Wide receiver Willie Green and I tried to drive to the Broncos' facility but his car got stuck. We shoveled him out, put his car in the garage and took my car. Once we got to the facility, we sat for four or five hours. We realized then that we were lucky. Some of the guys barely made it.

Everybody was stuck in the snow somewhere.

Finally, we piled on the team bus to make it to the airport. We had seen the news, seen the pile of wrecked cars on Pena Boulevard. It looked like a disaster zone. We didn't think we would even get near our plane. But we kept going.

As it turned out, our flight was the only flight allowed out of Denver's airport that day. It was delayed 12 hours. We made it to Buffalo after midnight, 12 hours before kickoff.

The NFL's position was clear.   Forget the danger we were in trying to get there, the risks involved in travel, or the fact that our families were scared to death. The league expected a game on Sunday.

All the players were furious. And all that rage was channeled into the game. I didn't play because of the artificial turf. Coach Shanahan gave me the day off because of my knee injury.

Sheer determination was our fuel.

But despite all of the madness, we beat the Bills 23-20 in OT.

This victory was an example of our determination, as well as our ability to focus and block out all other distractions. Our team had one goal in mind—to make it to the Super Bowl. End of story. Come hell or high water, and yes, even 10 feet of snow, we wanted to make it to the big game. The Buffalo win was evidence of our commitment to our goal.

Sheer determination was our fuel.

GRIFF NOTES

The Block

I've had several major obstacles to overcome throughout my life and career, but along the way, I learned to look at them as lessons. Once you recognize that blocks will appear, that no one is exempt, you can design your game plan in a way that helps you get over the hump.

You overcome blocks with

- **Determination**
- **Discipline**
- **Dedication**

Although it's inevitable that you will encounter some setbacks, distractions, and roadblocks, it's your reaction to them that determines the end result.

10   THE TACKLE

IN THE '96 SEASON, THE YEAR BEFORE I ARRIVED, the Broncos had clinched the AFC West title and home-field advantage through the playoffs on December 1. They had played three games—all of them easy wins—had a bye week in the first round of the playoffs, and then got ambushed by the Jacksonville Jaguars at home in Mile High Stadium.

They lost their first game in the playoffs. The Broncos were considered, at that time, the best team in the league. So that loss hit hard. It's a part of Broncos history that everyone in Denver will remember.

In '97, we were still proving ourselves. Elway didn't have a Super Bowl victory under his belt. And Mile High fans were having flashbacks of the Jacksonville loss, that devastating end to a solid season that many felt should have ended in a journey to the Big Game.

So, in order not to make the same mistake twice, everyone was talking about being focused, preparing, training, and studying. We couldn't go out there thinking that they we were indestructible.

The '97 season was an entirely different story. Making it to the playoffs was the first step.

GRIFF NOTE: *Plan for success, step by step.*

We had our work cut out for us. There would be no shortcuts, no easy wins, no skipping along to the Super Bowl. If we wanted it, we'd have to fight for it.

And it went down like this:

Oakland vs. Denver

We avenged the Oakland defeat at Mile High on November 24. We scored four times from inside the red zone, three of them on runs of two, three, and 19 yards. Terrell and I were playing exceptionally well in that game. We were definitely on the same page.

Kansas City vs. Denver

Next, we turned around and lost to the Kansas City Chiefs, 24-22, at Arrowhead Stadium when our defense allowed the Chiefs to march downfield in the final moments. Pete Stoyanovich's 54-yard field goal won the game for Kansas City as the clock ran out.

It was a dramatic ending to a game that could have gone either way. We certainly fought the good fight, but time had worked against us.

We found out later that we had achieved a franchise record: ten 100-yard rushing games by Terrell Davis, including two 200-yard efforts.

Off to Pittsburgh.

Pittsburgh vs. Denver

We played horribly during a 35-24 loss to the Pittsburgh Steelers at Three Rivers Stadium. This loss ultimately cost us home-field advantage throughout the AFC playoffs.

The Pittsburgh game is one I'll never forget. Personally, it was one of the worst games I'd ever had. I didn't execute a few plays as well as I should have; but worse than that, out of my own frustration, I had an exchange of words with one of their players, and that battle went on throughout the game.

After the game, one sports station claimed that the Steelers stopped Davis because I didn't get the job done. They showed footage of a play where Levon Kirkland flattened me. I was blamed for the Pittsburgh loss.

San Francisco vs. Denver

The following week we hit the skids during a 34-17 loss to the San Francisco 49ers on the ABC Monday Night game. Terrell suffered a mild shoulder separation, and Romanowski was caught on camera spitting in the face of J. J. Stokes, the young San Francisco wide receiver.

That was the second story reported on ESPN that night. ESPN's sportscasters compared it to the incident a couple of years before, when the Baltimore Orioles' Roberto Alomar Jr. spit in the face of umpire John Hirschbeck.

Things were looking so bleak for us at that point. And our Super Bowl dream started to fade.

Romanowski was shocked by the reaction, and even more shocked when people started saying it was a racist action.

Willie Green spoke for a lot of us when he said, "I don't care what color you are, I don't care *who* you are, it makes me angry to see a man disrespect another man by spitting in his face. That's what my parents taught me—you don't spit in anyone's face, you don't kick people."

Things were looking bleak for us at that point. And our Super Bowl dream started to fade.

The Denver newspapers made a huge deal out of the whole thing, which didn't surprise me. I saw it coming.   Growing up in Chicago, where the *Sun-Times* and the *Chicago Tribune* were constantly at war with each other, I expected a full-fledged media melee. The sports media had a field day with the "Romo controversy," painting a picture of animosity and defiance.

But what could any of us say? It happened on national television, in living color. And what you didn't see, you heard about.

I knew it looked bad. I also knew that the media wasn't going to let us forget it, at least not until they had juiced it to the fullest. The news coverage was disturbing. It was the kind of thing that could have easily distracted us and caused us to lose our focus. So we had to tackle the problem dead-on before it destroyed us as a team.

We had to tackle the problem dead-on before it destroyed us as a team.

I know Romo, and I know how charged up he gets out on the field. But I don't know why he made such an erratic move. It was wrong—plain and simple. I was mad at him, but he's still my teammate. So it wasn't just his problem, it was *our* problem.

The charges of racism, naturally, created tension. Considering the large number of black players on the team, and in the NFL, for that matter, we couldn't sit back and let it ride. We had to clear the air.

So a team meeting was called.

It was a "players only" meeting. And Elway spoke first, which was rare for him. In my time on the team, I hadn't ever seen him be the first to come forward in a team meeting. But this time was different, and I think he realized that it was important for him to lead the way. He set the tone for the meeting. He asked, "Are we going to let this divide us? Is this going to wreck our season?"

GRIFF NOTE: *Air out grievances.*

Lots of other players stood up and spoke their minds. It wasn't necessarily a confrontational meeting, but more of an open forum. Everyone was honest and straightforward. There was no beating around the bush. Since it was just us players, no one was worried about our discussion leaking to the press or to the coaches. We trusted each other and gave the floor to whoever had something to say. And we all listened.

"Are we going to let this divide us? Is this going to wreck our season?"

In the end, everyone said basically the same thing. The message was clear: It was the wrong move, but we could not, and would not, allow it to compromise all the work we had put into the season.

We decided to move on.

We turned our attention away from all the madness and directed it back to the playoff season. It didn't take long for us to get back on track. In our final regular-season game against San Diego, we won, 38-3, to finish the '97 season with a 12-4 record.

This was a decent record, but we were left without home-field advantage. In order to get to the Super Bowl, we had to win two games on the road. We were the wild card team. And our journey became known as "The Revenge Tour."

We kicked it off at Mile High with our old nemesis—the Jacksonville Jaguars.

Jacksonville vs. Denver

The Jacksonville game was a grudge match. The Jags have proven since their inception that they're determined to get better and better each year. Their organization is not afraid to go out and spend the money to bring in a player they feel is going to be a difference-maker. They have young players, and they are still adding to their arsenal. Each season they are a team to be reckoned with.

Against Jacksonville, we scored touchdowns on our first three possessions and led, 21-0, after 32 plays. Terrell had missed the final regular-season game with a slightly separated right shoulder. Yet he carried 31 times for 184 yards and two TDs. When he left late in the third quarter with bruised ribs, Derek Loville stepped in.

He'd just been promoted to second string because his backup, Vaughn Hebron, was nursing a strained left hamstring. Derek ran for 103 yards and scored two touchdowns in the fourth quarter. With both Terrell Davis and Derek Loville topping 100 yards, it marked only the third time in NFL postseason history that two backs on the same team gained 100 yards in a single game. The Broncos pounded out 310 yards on the ground, the fifth-best rushing performance in NFL postseason history.

We were back on track.

The win against Jacksonville set the pace for the next two games. You could feel the intensity and determination from all the guys on the team. You could see it in our eyes. We wanted a championship.

Headlines

Reprinted from *Sports Illustrated,* November 2, 1998, by Austin Murphy:

"*Meet Howard Griffith, the best blocking fullback, bar none. Against the Jaguars he touched the ball twice, on a pair of receptions, which is a lot for him. (Going into Sunday's game, he had two carries and six catches.) But he steamrolled one Jacksonville defender after another with his blocks. Griffith, a points machine as a senior at Illinois in 1990, when he had an NCAA-record eight touchdowns in one game, has scored seven times in his five-year pro career. He could care less about not getting the ball. A free agent who left the Carolina Panthers to sign with the Broncos before the '97 season, he embraces his role in Denver.*"

Kansas City, here we come.

Kansas City vs. Denver

The Chiefs were feeling good about themselves. Everybody figured they could dominate us. But the Chiefs underestimated our drive. We had lost to them a couple of weeks before, but not because we'd been out-executed. We just hadn't gotten the job done. When we lose a game, we face it head- on. We don't sit around and sugarcoat it.

We went ahead, 7-0, thanks to Terrell's one-yard run. The Chiefs scored 14 points in the third quarter, but Elway came back and hit McCaffrey for a 43-yard gainer to the 1-yard line, and Davis scored a few minutes later to give us a 14-10 lead.

> *We started to enjoy being on the road, ruining everybody's party.*

The Chiefs mounted one last drive that scared us for a minute.

But we held.

On to Pittsburgh.

We had played poorly in the last game against Pittsburgh. But we were a different team after the Kansas City win. And there was no way we were going to let them get the best of us this time. Too much was riding on the game.

At this point, we started to enjoy being on the road, ruining everybody's party.

Everyone was partying but me.

I remember in the locker room after the Kansas City win, I was getting dressed and Jason Elam could tell I was upset.

"Howard, what's wrong?"

"I'm just getting ready for No. 99."

Enough said.

I hadn't forgotten those accusations by one sports broadcaster who said I couldn't block, and that Levon Kirkland intimidated me. Intimidated? Levon's a great player, but…intimidated? Come on. I'm not intimidated by anyone. How did Terrell get 1,800 yards in a season? Did he get his yards when I was on the bench? They had insulted me, second-guessed my talent, and downplayed my effectiveness on the team.

I aimed to set the record straight.

SIDELINE

Terrell Davis,
Tailback, Denver Broncos

"There's a big weight difference between Kirkland and Howard. And a lot of times bad plays just happen. Lots of times I don't have the game I want, and I go back and look at how I could've done better. But it was eating away at Howard. You could just see it eating away at him. He was not going to let it happen again, even if Kirkland is huge."

AFC Championship Game
Pittsburgh vs. Denver

Everybody was angry before the Denver-Pittsburgh AFC Championship game. I was still fuming about media critiques of my game. The Steelers were fuming about the Broncos' critique of their game. After beating us, 35-24, weeks before, the Steelers believed that we had belittled their victory. Shanahan blamed the loss largely on a succession of dropped passes by his receivers, rather than a Steelers defense that held his team to three points in the second half.

Shanahan said the day after the defeat: "We had three passes dropped for 130 yards, and had another eight passes that were dropped that would have kept the momentum going. When you break it down and look at those opportunities, usually we make those. We had a chance to have a 500-yard game and we didn't get it done."

Elway said, "I threw the ball on the money. I get a little upset at the fact that it seems like every time we've been asked to answer the bell in big games, especially the last couple years, we haven't answered the bell. That's the frustrating thing, because good teams in big games play great. We haven't done that. I don't know if it's a psychological barrier. But we're not getting it done."

The Steelers posted these comments on their bulletin board with special emphasis on Shanahan's summations.

"The comments he made, he has to live with that," defensive end Kevin Henry said. "We're not going to let his comments get to us. These things happen in football, but when we lose, we don't make excuses, we just say, we lost the game."

As the psychological warfare heated up, I was determined to stay calm, which I didn't do in the previous game against Pittsburgh.

Those guys like to talk a lot of trash. It's part of their game. I got involved in it once, and it got me off my game. But in the second game, we got under Kirkland's skin. The whole game he was trying to get to me, constantly talking trash to me. "Howard," he said, "I can't believe they pay you all this money to do this." So I'm walking back to the huddle, we're still moving the ball up and down the field, and I'm feeling great.

I was determined to stay calm, which I didn't do in the previous game against Pittsburgh.

Oh, it's on now. It's actually fun to play under those circumstances, especially when you know you're prepared.

The Steelers had us on the back of our heels in the first half. Jerome Bettis ran right through us, and they built a 14-7 lead. But Ray Crockett came up with one of his timely interceptions. With 1:47 left in the half, we had a first down on Pittsburgh's 15, and I had a chance to redeem myself. I'd caught only 11 passes in the regular season, but Elway called for a flow pass to me in the left flat. I lined up to the left of Davis in the backfield. When Elway faked a handoff to Davis, I went to the line of scrimmage, and it looked as if I was going to be a blocker. Then I ran out to the left flat. At the same time, Ed McCaffrey ran a post pattern to remove Carnell Lake from the play. Shannon Sharpe ran a corner route to take in Darren Perry. And Davis' play-action fake fooled the linebackers, leaving me in the clear.

It was supposed to be an easy throw for John, but actually it's one of his most difficult, because I'm running away from him at full speed, and he's still dropping back. In other words, I have my back to him. Ninety-nine percent of the time, the pass is going to hit you in the back of your body. Elway flipped the ball behind me. I turned around and snagged it with one hand, then pulled it in as fast as possible.

I managed to do that . . . why stop there? Get in the end zone. Fast.

Just touch the pylon. Do that and you score.

Touchdown.

This score put us ahead to stay at 17-14. We could taste the Super Bowl.

Headlines

"Denver Broncos Fullback Howard Griffith," Reprinted from *Sports Spectrum* (Jan-Feb 1999) by Allen Palmeri:

"…Griffith's reward has been universal respect. 'He's going to do everything he possibly can to try to keep people off Terrell," says Pro Bowl tight end Shannon Sharpe. 'He realizes that his main job is to make sure Terrell does not get hit before he gets the ball and to give Terrell every opportunity he can to make big plays for us. He's done that.' 'Solid,' says cornerback Ray Crockett. 'Good character.' 'The best blocking fullback in football,' says Harry Swayne.

"Clearly the fifth option in Denver's offense, Griffith seldom rushes or receives. His total offense for the 1997 regular season was 89 yards. However, when quarterback John Elway needed him in the postseason, Griffith came up big. He turned a one-handed catch on a swing pass into a 15-yard touchdown against the Pittsburgh Steelers, giving the Broncos the lead for good in the AFC Championship Game…The defining statistic of Griffith's career is that three running back Jerome

Bettis in 1994, Anthony Johnson in 1996, and Davis in 1997—have enjoyed 1,000-yard seasons while sharing the backfield with him."

It was my first TD pass of the season. Even though my job is primarily blocking, every now and then, they throw me a bone. And that was a big bone. It was reminiscent of the touchdown I made at Carolina during the NFC championship, but this time it was sweeter. It was the most incredible play of my entire career.

Headlines

"Broncos and Packers reign…", Reprinted from *USA TO-DAY,* by Jarrett Bell (January 12, 1998):

"With Pittsburgh leading 14-10, Ray Crockett's end-zone interception with 4:40 left in the first half swung momentum. The Broncos marched 80 yards, capped by Howard Griffith's 15-yard touchdown grab, then took a 24-14 lead into halftime on Elway's 1-yard pass to Ed McCaffrey. 'Just like we've done all season,' said Broncos coach Mike Shanahan, 'we fought back.'

"The Broncos know what's next: the defending Super Bowl champion Green Bay Packers, favored to repeat.

"Said Elway, 'I want to go there and win one.'"

SIDELINE

Terrell Davis,
Tailback, Denver Broncos

"What makes Howard a great blocker is that he uses leverage. His angles are just phenomenal. He has a way of mixing his blocks up. He'll come in high one time and then cut the next time just to keep the guy off his feet. Mainly, he gets on the person and just stays on him. A lot of guys make great initial contact, then they lose the block. Howard's going to lock you up. You're not going anywhere.

"Another thing I like about Howard—he gets the ball and he goes to the hole quickly. He doesn't hesitate and try to read it like a halfback would. He gets up close to the line to take a shot. If he misses, that's great because the person isn't supposed to be where he is—he's not in the hole. Howard and I came a long way that season, and it paid off when we took off to the Super Bowl."

We were Super Bowl bound.

But once again, I wasn't in a party mood. I was still not happy about being singled out as the weak link. I was still on the defensive. I told reporters after winning the AFC title: *They woke a sleeping giant.*

I fired back on the media, letting them know that their attacks on me were unfounded. Up until that regular-season game against Pittsburgh, I was considered one of the top fullbacks in the league. Well, where did all of the talent go so suddenly? I believed their reporting of that game was

> **GRIFF NOTE:** *Defend your position.*

reckless and irresponsible. They picked out that one play as being the difference-maker in the game, but in the process, they decided it was all right to insult my intelligence and my skills as a football player. Analysis is one thing, criticism is one thing, but insults and personal blows to an athlete's skill and talent is hitting below the belt. I further tackled the problem through performance. I added the final note by demonstrating exactly what kind of player I am. Kirkland wasn't even a factor in the playoff game. Although in the regular-season game, the Steelers had held us to a season low of 89 yards, we pounded out 150 yards in the playoff game.

I will remember that game for a long time.

It was the end of the "Revenge Tour."

GRIFF NOTES

The Tackle

Overcoming obstacles and tackling your problems head on takes work but is well worth the effort. In the long run, you become stronger and more effective as a player and as a team.

In a team situation, always

- Communicate with teammates any problems or issues that stand to disrupt team effectiveness

- Air out your grievances

- Be honest and direct

- Being willing to move past problems and focus on team goals

When confronted with personal attacks or attacks on your team's character, performance, or reputation, you tackle that problem best through example. It's like the old adage: The proof is in the pudding. Show them what you've got and what you're made of. Success is the best defense.

Super Bowl XXXII

San Diego, California

GREEN BAY PACKERS VS. DENVER BRONCOS

Qualcomm Stadium

JANUARY 25,1998

THE GREEN BAY PACKERS LOBBED A COUPLE BOMBS into the Broncos' camp during the manic buildup to Super Bowl XXXII. On the Wednesday before the game, Packers offensive coordinator, Sherman Lewis, made the statement, publicly, that Elway wouldn't rank among football's greatest players unless he won a Super Bowl.

Then, Green Bay general manager Ron Wolf followed by saying: "If a quarterback hasn't won a Super Bowl, I would think he wouldn't deserve to be in the Hall of Fame. That's my opinion."

Everyone predicted we would lose.

The consensus was that Green Bay was going to send us packing. I couldn't understand it. Hadn't they been looking at film? Didn't they notice how well we had performed in the playoffs? Didn't they think we were going to do everything in our power to take home that trophy?

For a team like us, looking for an edge, Green Bay's cavalier regard for Elway, as well for our offensive line, was just what the doctor ordered. It gave us an edge and made them more vulnerable.

Again, never underestimate the opposition.

Brett Favre was playing great at that point. The defense was doing all the things it needed to do. So the hype was huge. The media bought into the Packer mystique . . . *and so did the Packers.*

It kept building.

In their interviews with the media, they took turns disrespecting us. They spoke about the Broncos' organization with total disregard. It was reckless on their part, because no matter

Never underestimate the opposition.

who you're playing, you have to maintain a level of respect for your opponent. What amazed me was the assumption that our offensive line couldn't deal with the Packers' defense. After all, we'd put up so many impressive numbers over 16 regular-season

Ego—it all boiled down to ego.

games and three playoff victories. But you would have thought we didn't have even the slightest chance at beating them. The Packers had Reggie White and Gilbert Brown, end of story.

But we had our own story to tell.

We couldn't figure out why so many people were counting us out before we even got there. They weren't just picking us to lose, they were picking us to get blown out. They put us on the defensive. Although we weren't defending a title, we were defending our solid reputation, not to mention all the hard work we had put into the regular season and the playoffs.

Ego—it all boiled down to ego.

The Packers started believing their own press releases. In this business, there are players who talk trash just to bring attention to themselves. Some parlay all that talk into a big endorsement deal or a picture on a cereal box. Everyone's got an agenda. Then, there are others who talk all that stuff to send you on a head-trip, and plant seeds of doubt in the minds of their opponent. And let's face it, the Super Bowl is the big stage, the perfect place to act out.

Millions of people watch the Super Bowl. The tiny air bases in Kuwait watch it. It is watched in Europe. With high technology, satellites, and the Internet, it has become a global event.

So it's easy to get seduced by the whole scene.

What some players don't understand is that the media is just standing by waiting for a spectacle. If you say something positive, you may get a little airtime, but start talking crazy, and your face and name will be spread all over the nightly news. Reporters know exactly who to approach to get sensational stories. It's a game of cat and mouse. But you've got to be smarter than that. If you're going to open your mouth, you've got to be able to back up what you're saying. It's up to you to control the interview.

Take Shannon Sharpe. Shannon knows exactly what he's doing when he makes wild statements to the press. He is fully aware of the consequences, because he can just about measure the reaction. But Shannon, no matter what, always stands by his word. He never backs out of his statements. And you've got to respect that.

There's something alluring about being in the hot seat,

If you're going to open your mouth, you've got to be able to back up what you're saying.

knowing that you can say whatever you want, let off steam, or resist the temptation to spout a lot of negativity. It's dangerous ground.

Also, 1997 was a particularly tough time to play against the Green Bay Packers. Brett Favre is playing great, Reggie White is a legend, Gilbert Brown is the largest guy in football, and their defense is playing hard. So the hype is swirling. In most of their interviews, you could sense their confidence.

Meanwhile, the Broncos remained focused. We kept a low profile throughout the events leading up to the Super Bowl. We only conducted media interviews that were scheduled. And we kept our composure, kept practicing, and stayed focused.

We didn't fall for any of the hype, though they piled it on thick. They said our offense couldn't run against them because every one of their defensive linemen weighed roughly 30 pounds more than each of our offensive linemen. We don't have a guy who's 300 pounds. We've played against guys who are that big, and it hasn't been a problem. We're going to run right at them, and the most conditioned athletes are going to win.

I was given a video camera by ESPN to document the Broncos' Super Bowl journey, mostly behind-the-scenes stuff. Once we knew we were going, that week, I started taping. I taped footage of the day we flew to San Diego, with all of the guys suited up, getting on the plane. It was an exciting time for us. Our underdog status, in some ways, helped us relax and keep things in perspective. We were honestly just happy to have made it to the Super Bowl. For many of our players, it was their first Super Bowl experience. We wanted to win, of course, and had prepared to win, but we weren't about to miss the entire experience by worrying or becoming anxious.

One of our biggest considerations for Super Bowl XXXII was John Elway. We weren't just playing to get ourselves Super Bowl rings, but to get John his ring. The Denver Broncos were John's team. There's no question about it. We have a lot of veterans and All-Pros on the team, but everyone knows Denver is John's town.

I remember John being calm and relaxed. He was happy to have had another opportunity to win a Super Bowl. He had suffered

> *We were honestly just happy to have made it to the Super Bowl.*

losses in the past, along with all of the negative press that went along with them. He was focused. This was his chance to put an end to all the talk about the one thing lacking from his stellar career.

When we arrived in San Diego, we stayed out of the public eye as much as possible. We had pretty strict curfews. None of us spent much time with our families. Our wives and kids weren't allowed to stay in the same room with us the day before the game. There was a lot of security around the hotel. You had to have a password just to get a phone call through to the hotel operator. At one point, we were using the freight elevators in the back of the hotel just to get in and out, because the frenzy in the Hyatt lobby never died down.

I had a lot of family members come down to support me. My son stayed back in Chicago with my mother-in-law, and my wife, Kim, hung out with her sister and some of our other friends from Chicago. My stepmother, Joy, has family in the San Diego area, so she visited with them. And I think of the entire group, my dad and father-in-law, who had roomed together, had more fun than anyone.

...everyone knows Denver is John's town.

I heard, after the fact, that they were always missing in action. They came home with more stories and more photos than anyone else.

The Super Bowl experience is a great time for the players' families. And it's good to know that your folks are settled in, socializing and having a good time, because on the flip side, the pressure on the players is incredible. It's difficult to concentrate on anything other than the game.

Just when you thought the media hype couldn't get any bigger, they turn it up a few more notches. So many things are running through your mind. It's the Super Bowl—that other world you've spent your whole life dreaming about, and now . . . here you are.

The way sports are covered these days, you're under the microscope the entire time, particularly on game day. So it's possible that you'll go down in history for anything memorable or out of the ordinary. A dropped pass, a missed block, a blocked field goal, whatever—that's how you will be remembered. No one cares how hard you had to work to get there. It no longer matters. Take Thurman Thomas—he will be remembered for missing the first couple of plays in the Super Bowl against Washington back in '91 because he couldn't find his helmet. Scott Norwood will be remembered for missing the potential game-winning field goal in the Super Bowl against the New York Giants.

Choking is everyone's worst fear.

Take a guy like Bill Buckner when he was playing first base for the Boston Red Sox. He was a great player but he'll be remembered on tape with the ball rolling through his legs in the World Series. And that's one of the ironies about professional sports— even college sports.

Choking is everyone's worst fear.

No matter how great you are, one false move and your reputation is marred, your foul-up etched in stone, caught on film, and preserved in the archives.

The anxiety is unbelievable. How did I handle it? I didn't sleep the night before the game. I slept the morning of the game. The fear factor, the anxiety, kept me awake the night before. I tossed and turned, tried to watch the television, listened to music. I sat there looking at the TV but not really watching. I wasn't worried about lack of sleep. Once you step on the field, you're blood is pumping at such a high level, the lack of sleep doesn't even affect you.

When I went to sleep in the days leading up to the Super Bowl, I was looking at my game plan, replaying the game all the time in my mind. Before I played the game, I was playing the game in my head. So much of what I do depends on my making split-second judgments and quick adjustments. I have to know not only what my initial assignment is, but also what I have to do to execute it.

It's funny because people start getting superstitious when so much is riding on the game. You'll pull out an old rabbit's foot if you have one. It's all nerves. I re-

> *One false move and your reputation is marred . . . and preserved in the archives.*

member the first time we walked into the stadium on media day. Now, up to that point, Terrell's locker has always been on my right, but somehow that day, he ended up on my left. I looked around and I said, "Whoa, whoa, wait a minute, man. We have to change this. Terrell, you belong on this side. Get over here."

Terrell's thing is he gets to the stadium exactly at call time, not a minute earlier. Shannon Sharpe wears the same hat to Saturday-night meetings. A baseball cap—I think it's the only one he wears. Harold Hasselbach always has to get to the stadium on game day very early. He has to be one of the first players there so he can go in the training room and chop up the ice in the

I have to know not only what my initial assignment is, but what I have to do to execute it.

cold tub. That's his thing. Nobody puts the ice in the ice cooler until Harold gets there.

Then there are others who take the same route all the way to practice or to the airport. They park in the same side of the airport; even if the flight is flying out of the west side, they'll still park on the east side. Thinking back to college, for four years I sat in the same seat in team meetings. It could be superstition, or it could be that we're all creatures of habit.

I have to put my pants on just right and not too early. I have to get my hamstrings rubbed first. Then one of the last things I do, which always makes me late, is tape my wrists. So everybody is ready to go, and there I am taping my wrists. I wait until the last minute. The whole time, I'm looking at the playbook. If I could, I'd take it out on the field with me. Every chance I get, I'm trying to find that extra edge. But on game day, I go over the reminder sheet that Coach Kubiak gives out. That's a point of contention among a lot of coaches. They ask, "Why do you give them scripts? They can't take the scripts out there on Sunday?" But the Broncos believe if that's the way some players prefer to get ready, let them.

Coach Shanahan—you usually see him pacing if he's nervous about a game. If you see him walking around the locker room, circling, going back and forth, you know he's anxious to play the game. He might get involved in a little small talk, but

> *Every chance I get, I'm trying to find that extra edge.*

mostly he's quiet and pacing. I suppose for a coach, game day is probably more nerve-racking because at that point, they've done all they can do. It's out of their hands. The rest is up to us.

Coach Bobby Turner, our running-back coach—he'll come and get our tests. We have a little ritual, too. Vaughn Hebron used to turn in his test on Saturday night at our team meeting. The rest of us turn in our tests when we get to the stadium. So Coach Turner comes and gets everybody's tests, then he goes and sits in the bathroom, right outside the showers, and goes over his game plan. He's in there the whole time. He's always going back and forth studying personnel. If a guy is hurt, then he's coaching the guy who'll replace him. Last- minute notes. He tries to do everything he can to give his players an edge, or, as he calls it, "food." And on game day, he wants everyone to be completely full.

On Super Bowl Sunday, the locker room was more frenetic than usual. Some guys were videotaping. There were video cameras going all over the place—on the bus, in the locker room—everywhere. Finally, somebody screamed, "Turn off the tape! We have plenty of time for that afterwards!"

Everybody wanted to capture the moment. Because, hey, you don't know if you'll have the chance again. Who knows if you are going to make it back to another Super Bowl? It's history in the making.

Terrell and I were pretty normal. We were just sitting there, hanging out. But we kept having to go to the bathroom. We call it "the coward." So I'm coming out and here he comes. "Oh, man, the coward's got me."

Elway was joking with Bubby. My teammates were in their own small groups, going over plays. You heard all of these conversations:

"What happens with this play?"

"What do I need to look for?"

When it was time to go out on the field, I started reflecting on my past—my parents, my family, and all of the hard work that led up to that day. It was an overwhelming moment. You realize that you have the chance to be the greatest team in football for that particular year—if you can just go out and win this one game. You also think about not tripping over all of those wires on the field when your name is called during the introduction. There were wires everywhere in San Diego. We were literally running over them to get onto the field. And if you fell, it would be caught on film. So I was saying to myself:

Don't trip over the wires! Please.

Then the thought occurred to me:

"Turn off that tape! We have plenty of time for that afterwards!"

Man, do you know where you are? This is the Super Bowl.

Sure, you see it during the week before the game. You hear all of the Super Bowl buildup. You're buying tickets, everybody's calling you, the media are talking about the match up. But it set in when we were standing in the tunnel, waiting for our introductions. When I heard my name called—that was a defining moment in my life. The feeling, the rush, the sense of pride you feel is completely breathtaking. There are so many feelings racing through your body, and no two people have the same exact feelings. It's an individual thing. You are part of the biggest sporting event in the world, moments away from the opportunity to be ranked "the best."

In fact, the appropriate reaction to all of that is to either scream

> *When I heard my name called—that was a defining moment in my life.*

and shout or just break down crying, but because football is a tough guy's game, and winning is the plan, you put on your game face and run out on the field.

Understandably, every player has to feel that sense of anxiety and elation. I remember Joe Montana once said that he actually hyperventilated when the national anthem was sung. It is such a special moment that there are no words to fully describe it.

Once the game clock started, all anxieties were pushed aside. It was time to do what we came to do. Win the game.

The Packers had the ball. They scored on their first drive.

We didn't panic.

It goes back to believing in the system, believing in your game plan, and trusting the guys playing next to you. We weren't worried about it.

The beginning of the game did little to dent Green Bay's confidence. We stuffed Dorsey Levens on his first run, and Brett Favre didn't complete his first pass. But on third down, Favre managed to deal with a blitz to hit Antonio Freeman for a 13-yard gain.

It was off to the races for the rest of the drive. Between Levens' running and Favre's passing, we couldn't do much to stop them from going up, 7-0.

You could just hear people saying, "Here we go again. Another Super Bowl meltdown for the Broncos."

Again, we didn't panic. In fact, since I've been here, we've never doubted our ability to answer the call.

Who gets the credit? We all do. If one guy panics, the rest *The feeling, the rush, the sense of pride you feel is completely breathtaking.* may go with him. We couldn't control what Green Bay did on offense. But we could move the ball ourselves.

We put together a 12-play scoring drive, with Terrell running and me blocking, six times. He scored on a one-yard drive, marking the first time in Super Bowl history that a team had scored on

its first possession after its opponent had scored on its first posses-

sion.

Shanahan's planning was flawless for that game. We found

plays that capitalized on Green Bay's vulnerabilities. Those plays are

the difference-mak-

ers, because anytime   *If one guy panics, the rest*

you can put points   *may go with him.*

on the board, momentum shifts. Every play makes a huge differ-

ence. And in a Super Bowl, you've only got one game to win. You

can't come back and try to recoup the following next week.

No one figured we'd run the ball in Reggie White's direction.

No team was supposed to have the nerve to do that. But why avoid

him? That's the worst possible game plan. The worst thing you can

do against a great defensive player is to run away from him. When

you run at him, you force him into decisions. He might make a

play here and there, but your chances are greater when you're run-

ning at him than when you're running away. You're more in con-

trol.

Still, our defense had its back against the wall. It couldn't

allow another routine scoring drive. Instead of playing it safe, our

defense threw everything at the Packers, which was the safest way to

go.

So what happened?

Tyrone Braxton intercepted a Favre pass on Green Bay's second possession, which gave us the ball near midfield.

Our offensive line was destroying the Packers, and we took off on a 55-yard scoring drive. Did it surprise me that the Packers' defense began to wilt? No. We were superbly conditioned, the day was humid, and our offensive line had a little grudge to settle.

It was time to even the score.

Elway scored on a one-yard run. Davis didn't get the call, because a few plays before, he'd been kicked in the head. He was on the sideline, unable to see. We found out later that he hadn't taken his anti-migraine medication at the right time earlier that day, so he was overcome by a blinding migraine.

Anytime you can put points on the board, momentum shifts.

Shanahan called a time-out and asked Davis if he could return to the game as a decoy for what became Elway's scoring run.

I saw Terrell on the sideline. But, at the time, I didn't know why he wasn't in the game. I didn't know until I came over and looked at him that he was having trouble. It wasn't a matter of, "Can he run the next play?" The question was, "Will we get Terrell back?"

We had to keep moving. Every once in a while, I'd check on him, but it was critical that we stick to our game plan. Af-

> *It wasn't a matter of "Can he run the next play?" The question was, "Will we get Terrell back?"*

ter all, this was the Super Bowl.

Looking back, what's funny about that "decoy play" is that Terrell said he couldn't see. But if you look at the film, there's a Packer coming right at him, low, and Terrell managed to avoid him. So, whether he had blurred vision or not, he was determined to stay sharp.

Jason Elam then kicked a long field goal before the half. But the Packers came right back with a 95-yard scoring march.

We could have been in a big jam at this point, because we weren't sure of Terrell's status. The stats were against us—we hadn't scored in the third quarter in three playoff wins, and Elway had thrown for 27 yards in the first half. But we still led, 17-14.

On the first play of the second half, I believe Terrell fumbled.

But our defense came forward, holding the Packers to a field goal. A little bit later, we took over on our own 8-yard line. And that's when we kicked into high gear. A couple of passes to Ed McCaffrey, some big runs by Terrell, and we moved to Green Bay's 12.

The Packers were fading.

On third down, Elway dropped back to pass, saw Reggie White coming for his head, stepped out of his way, and took off for the goal line. He avoided another tackle, but as three Packers came for the big kill, he got flipped around in a midair collision and was spun around like a helicopter. But he came down with a first down.

It was incredible.

Anytime John gets hit like that, you say, "Oh, no!" But it worked. It was evidence of John's desire to win the game. The adrenaline was flowing after that. We were all hyped.

Elway tried to gun down the Packers on the next possession. A mistake? Not at all. John wanted it. He had the Packers bleeding, and he wanted to go in for the kill. Besides, that's the way Elway plays. He's a gunslinger. He wouldn't be John Elway if he didn't take chances.

My turn came when I rushed once for two yards and caught one pass for a 23-yard gain, giving us a first down at the Green Bay 8-yard line in the closing minutes of the third quarter. The play was identical to the one where I scored the TD in the AFC championship game against Pittsburgh.

In the fourth quarter, we went 49 yards for another score. When John Mobley stepped in front of Brett Favre's final pass, sheer hysteria overcame our sideline. Coach Bobby Turner was going nuts, like he usually does in big games. Everyone was congratulating Shanahan. The clock was ticking in our favor. The defense was on the field at that point, but we got the ball back because the Packers had turned it over on downs. Since Green Bay didn't get a first down, our offense had to go back out on the field. Funny thing is, at that point, some of us already had on our championship caps. In all of the excitement, some guys ran out there with their caps on, and forgot their helmets. That's just how excited we were.

SIDELINE

Kim Griffith,
Howard's wife

"During the game, I told my mother-in-law, 'If they win, I'm going down on the field.' I remember watching past Super Bowl games on television, and the end of the game always seemed so exciting. There's the confetti falling and balloons, all the family members running out on the field. Well, I knew that I wanted to be a part of all of that. It was Howard's turn to play and my turn to really cheer him on, in a big way.

"Once the final minutes ran off the clock, I was on my way. I told my family not to wait for me if they didn't make it on the field. I would just meet them back at the hotel. I was determined to get down there and find Howard to congratulate him. Of course, security didn't want to let anyone down on the field unless the player had come to get them. But Howard was swamped by the media, and didn't even realize I was trying to get on the field. Nevertheless, I got down there. I remember Alfred Williams told the security guard to let me over, after he had just helped his wife over the gate.

"So I jumped down, and I do mean jumped down, onto the field, heels and all, and surprisingly enough, I spotted Howard in all of that mania. We caught each other's eye in the midst of the madness and I went over to congratulate him. He was being interviewed by a sports reporter, but I just stood there on that field next him in the middle of everything, thrilled to death."

When the clock ran out, there was total mayhem. Confetti was flying, the scoreboards were shooting out smoke, and people were running out onto the field. The field was immediately filled with cameramen, sports reporters, and family members.

My wife ran down onto the field. She was ecstatic. And my dad was the proud father. It was as much fun for him as it was for me, which is why I always insist that I'm not playing just for myself.

There are so many people you bring with you every time you walk out onto a field.

There was hollering and screaming, tears of joy, cameras flashing, cameras rolling.   It was off the hook.

The Denver Broncos had won their first Super Bowl championship.

DENVER	7	10	7	7	31
Green Bay	7	7	3	7	24

It was one of the greatest feelings in the world. There is nothing to compare it to, because it is unlike anything I've ever experienced.

Everybody was so excited that we had finally done it. You sweat and bleed with these guys, and to reach the ultimate goal together is incredible.

Emotions were riding high in the locker room.

I remember that in the midst all of the cheers and congratulations, Rod Smith was going berserk on a media guy: "You didn't pick us to win!" he was screaming. "Why are you in our locker room now? You didn't think we could win, so why do you want to celebrate with us now?"

All of the angst and anxiety that we had been suppressing throughout the playoffs caused all kinds of reactions. We had been walking around with all that pressure the week leading up the Super Bowl, so when the lids came off…people cut loose.

Meanwhile, I was thinking about all the people who said I'd never make it. I remembered all the teams I'd left behind. I realized that this was a huge accomplishment for me, personally, but also for all of the people I'm close to in my life. It's a big, big deal.

I especially thought of my mom, who never got to see me play football.

SIDELINE

Karen Chilton,
Howard's sister-in-law

"I will never forget the look on Howard's face when he walked into the big party that night at the Hyatt, hours after the game. It is really indescribable. He had this fantastic smile on his face. He looked like a five-year-old at Christmas. And after all the autographs and the picture taking, the dinner, the laughs, and even the silences, I thought: This is really incredible—to witness someone in his moment of glory. To watch him achieve his biggest and wildest dream. What a sight! It was fantastic."

SIDELINE

Chick Harris
Running-Back Coach, Carolina Panthers

"I was so elated. All of us were in the race for the Super Bowl championship, but once we were out of it and Howard continued to go out and win it, it was like me winning it. See, it transcends more than just him as a player wearing the colors of my team. It's a young man who's gone from Indianapolis to Buffalo to San Diego . . . who I first saw on a hot summer day in a scrimmage with the L.A. Rams . . . I'm looking at a kid who I'm thinking is Natrone Means, and it's Howard Griffith. And he's a running back, not a fullback, then we get him in L.A., and all of a sudden he has to be a good fullback for us with good running ability. But he learned the position. He learned the system. It wasn't always easy for him, but he stayed the course. And I was so happy to see a culmination of all that hard work and determination get him to the Super Bowl. He got there before I did. And if I'm not ever able to get there, I'll always feel good about him carrying the flag into the championship. I'll feel that somehow I had a part in it."

SIDELINE

Randall Townsel,
Friend/Former Julian Football Player

"The win was the icing. But the cake was Howard being there. When someone who's from where you're from gets to that level, gets to a Super Bowl, that's a dream come true for everybody. It was for Coach J. W. Smith and the whole fraternal order of Julian High School football. For all of the football players that didn't get there, Howard got there for all of us. I was so happy for him."

When you consider our overall performance in the Super Bowl, I believe we were right on in that game. We stuck to our game plan and executed well. Of course, there were plays that could have been done better, but in the grand scheme of things, we did extremely well. I feel confident that I did my part from an offensive position in contributing to the win. In terms of my individual performance, I think I'd rank myself about an 8 on a scale of 1 to 10. There are certain plays that I feel I executed well. One was the goal-line play where I was going after Butler, and while I got twisted by another guy, I still tried to block. I don't even know how I did it. It was sheer determination. I remember backing up, pushing him, and getting him out of the way. There was another play I remember when we were going around again, and I knocked Williams down, which allowed Terrell to go down field for a long gain.

It was a real guts-and-glory game.

Terrell was Super Bowl MVP.

Elway was in his glory.

And the Denver Broncos had evened the score.

GRIFF NOTES

The Score

Before the Super Bowl, the Denver Broncos adopted this attitude:

We don't want to just score on the field, or make a good showing, we want to dominate.

Now, obviously, we're not able to dominate every team we play against, but that authoritative stance puts you on the right track to win the Big Game. You become a force to be reckoned with.

In any major competition, confidence is the key. You must go in believing that you can win, that you deserve to win, and that you will win.

12 THE WIN

"THIS IS GOING TO BE THE SHORTEST OFF-SEASON EVER," one of the guys said.

None of us knew just how much hoopla surrounded a Super Bowl victory. The phone was ringing nonstop, the fax machine was overflowing; everybody wanted an interview, wanted you to do a radio show, a TV spot, an autograph session, a charity event.

When we arrived back in Denver, there was a huge championship parade, which was a first for me. People were nine and 10 deep throughout the parade route. It was amazing to see that many people show up to congratulate the team. I think after seeing all of the fans out there waving Broncos paraphernalia, screaming and shouting, our victory set in. All of us were on top of the world.

When my family and I packed up and went home for the off-season, my wife threw me a big party in Chicago. All of our friends and family who couldn't make it to the actual game were able to share in some of the joy. Everybody was so excited. We had a tape of the game playing in the suite, music, food, champagne, a Super Bowl cake, the whole thing.

SIDELINE

Quintin Parker, Former Illinois Strong Safety

"I didn't go to the game, but I was there in San Diego. I was staying with Frank Hartley, who played with us at Illinois. Frank was playing for San Diego at the time and his place was about five minutes from the stadium. We were all about to get kicked out of his apartment complex for making so much noise. When the Broncos won the Super Bowl, for me, it was just an incredible feeling to see someone close to you accomplish something that huge. Every kid, no matter who they are, from the time they start playing football, they want to be the world champion. And to see someone that you know do it, as far as I'm concerned, that was like all of us doing it. We were all like, "Hey, *Griff got it*.""

I played in several golf outings and made personal appearances all summer long. When you win a Super Bowl, everybody wants a piece of you…and that's a good thing.

SIDELINE

Henry Jones,
Defensive Back, Buffalo Bills

"I was watching the '97 Super Bowl in Frank Hartley's apartment in San Diego with friends. I was happy for Howard and proud that one of our own Illini had won the big one. But at the same time, I reflected back on my three Super Bowl losses and wondered what it would be like to be on the winning side just once."

It has become customary in recent years for Super Bowl champions to visit the White House. This was an extraordinary experience, not so much because we were able to shake hands with the President, but because we were able to witness all of the pomp and circumstance surrounding the American presidency. It was interesting. Because there are so many players on football teams, we are given maybe 15 or 20 minutes of meeting time.

The day we met President Clinton, we were in and out in a matter of minutes. We were taken to the state dining room, that's where we waited for him to finish his business for the day. Then, we were ushered in with military-like precision:

"OK, bring the team over."

"OK, get against the wall."

"Back up."

"Wait."

So there we were, lined up against the wall. When the president began making his way through, everybody stopped moving. Apparently, this is the custom. No one moves when the president walks on the first floor of the White House. He came through, greeted all of the players and shook hands. He had more to say, naturally, to John Elway and Terrell Davis and even Steve Atwater, who had played at Arkansas, than he did to guys, let's say, on the practice squad. After he greeted us, we were moved to the pressroom. He gave a two-minute speech, took a couple of pictures—then he was gone.

I believe he said to me, "How are you doing? Congratulations." It was all in a day's work for him. And don't get me wrong, it was a privilege to meet him. It's an interesting minute…but it is just a minute.

With appearances, workouts, and camp, preseason came around faster than ever. It was as if we had no off-season. Before you knew it, it was time to go back to work.

At that time, we felt we were the best team in the league. We had a great roster and had every intention of going back into the regular season full force. However, no one could have predicted that we'd be undefeated by midseason, with the pressure mounting and everyone watching to see if we could actually do it.

Could we make it through the entire season undefeated?

In all of our media appearances, most of the players and coaches were busy saying that we weren't concerned with being an undefeated team, but the farther we went, the more speculation there was. We were under a microscope the entire season—everyone waiting for that one mishap, that one play that would ruin the record, spoil the show. Naturally, the fans wanted to see it happen. There hadn't been an undefeated regular season since the Miami Dolphins went 14-0 in '72. And in the media, it was as if they had nothing else to discuss, except:

Can the Denver Broncos be beaten?

No matter what the predictions, we had no other choice but to take it one game at a time.

Could we make it through the entire season undefeated?

SCORECARD 1998

Denver Broncos	27	New England Patriots	21
Denver Broncos	42	Dallas Cowboys	23
Denver Broncos	34	Oakland Raiders	17
Denver Broncos	38	Washington Redskins	16
Denver Broncos	41	Philadelphia Eagles	16
Denver Broncos	21	Seattle Seahawks	16
Denver Broncos	37	Jacksonville Jaguars	24
Denver Broncos	33	Cincinnati Bengals	26
Denver Broncos	27	San Diego Chargers	10
Denver Broncos	30	Kansas City Chiefs	7
Denver Broncos	40	Oakland Raiders	14
Denver Broncos	31	San Diego Chargers	16
Denver Broncos	35	Kansas City Chiefs	31
Denver Broncos	16	New York Giants	20
Denver Broncos	21	Miami Dolphins	31
Denver Broncos	28	Seattle Seahawks	21

New England vs. Denver

We started off the regular season with a game against New England. We wanted to get off to a fast start because we were of the mind-set that we'd make it back to the Super Bowl. A win against New England served as a good yardstick for our preparedness because the Patriots were solid on all sides of the ball.

Personally, I came back to the game lighter than I had been in the previous season. I felt if I added some speed to my game, it could give our team that extra edge. I already had the technique; the speed just enhanced it. I was questioned about it constantly.

Every off-season I think of ways to improve my game.

People were wondering: "Can he get the job done at that weight?" Even Terrell wondered. But there was a method to my madness. Every off-season I think of ways to improve my game. After the Super Bowl victory, I was particularly careful not to become complacent and lay back. Instead, I thought about ways in which we as a team could be even better.

Dallas vs. Denver

Our next game was against Dallas. Playing against Dallas was a big thrill. The Cowboys have so much talent on their team. When you have a chance to play against guys of that caliber, it's always an extra challenge. They have a rich tradition, and that's where every franchise wants to be. Dallas is considered "America's team."

I enjoy watching them, especially guys I have a lot of respect for, like recent retiree Darryl "Moose" Johnston who brought the fullbacks back into the fold. He played the game a little differently than I do. He liked to use a cut block because of his injuries. I like to take on guys as much as I can. All things being equal, it's always a good feeling playing against guys you respect, guys like "Moose," who've contributed so much to the game.

Although they have so much team speed, when you're playing against a guy like Terrell Davis, everybody wants to make a play. The problem is, you still have defensive assignments that indicate where you're supposed to be. Some opponents feel they can go over the top and make a play or come underneath and make a play; but in the process of doing that, they leave a seam wide open. Then we're able to get our receivers downfield and do a good job of blocking so they're out of position. And anytime the opponents are out of position, it's going to make what Terrell does even easier.

Our offensive line was so skilled that one step in the wrong direction or one false read by a linebacker made the difference between his making a stop for a one-yard gain, and his being completely out of position, thus allowing Terrell to go the distance.

Although I don't think Dallas was 100 percent that day, no one can deny that it is a team that's blessed with great players. You get a chance to play against guys like that, and it's a high note in your career, no matter what the outcome.

We were stacking up victories, one after the other, and even more speculation started to stir: *Can anyone beat Denver?*

Oakland vs. Denver

In Oakland, Elway was limping. At first, it didn't look bad but when a player grabs the back of his leg, immediately you know it's a hamstring. The next question is: How bad is it? He tried to stretch it out, but it didn't loosen up. When John left the field, everyone had to step up. When you are trying to win a championship, you realize that the unexpected happens. So you immediately get your backup ready, and he's got to come in and play big. In a game situation, when the game momentum has already been established, that player has to be so effective that we're not slowed down

> *Nobody wants to be the guy to slow the wagon down.*

and as little disruption as possible takes place during the transition. This is where knowledge of the game, as well as the game plan, comes into play. It is so easy for the offense to be stymied because the backup hasn't paid close-enough attention to the action on the field.

Bubby Brister was our backup.

Bubby is a tough guy. He's going to give you everything he's got. Again, nobody wants to be the guy to slow the wagon down. And Bubby has got that fire—he can't wait to get out there. Bubby has played for some teams where coaches didn't want that fire, didn't want him grabbing his players and yelling at officials. It wasn't a problem for us because, as far as we're concerned, that's Bubby. We can't ask him to come in and do something that's not him, especially at this stage in his career. He has proven that he can win games. You just have to let players go out and play. He's going to do whatever it takes to win a football game.

When Bubby came into the game against Oakland, he threw an interception on the first play. But we didn't panic. Ironically, it was probably one of the best things that could have happened to him at that moment. He demonstrated just how much of himself he was willing to lay on the line in order to win, and after that, everyone rallied behind him—his teammates, the media, and the fans. In many ways, it took the pressure off, and he was able to concentrate, calm down, and focus. After that play, we were able to move the ball. Then everybody jumped on the bandwagon because he showed that he could run the offense.

I remember the touchdown lob he threw to me. I was bumped by a rushing linebacker who was coming up the field, so instead of Bubby making an easy throw, he actually had to lob it over the guy's head so deep in the backfield that I needed to turn in a different direction in order to catch it. Bubby just laid it out there, allowing me to make the play on the ball. That was just one indication of his leadership ability and knowledge of the game.

He ended up throwing for 140 yards and two touchdowns in that game. We won, 34-17.

Winning that game against Oakland left us feeling good about ourselves. We had stepped up to our expected level of play when unexpected circumstances threatened to undermine our effort.

In the following game, there was a great deal of pressure on Bubby. He was just starting to get comfortable, though all of the media attention he was getting had to be distracting. Bubby had to get the game plan down, juggle interviews, undergo constant questioning and close scrutiny. He'd leave the practice field, and there would be 20 cameras watching him. He'd been in the situation where he was the main guy but this was slightly different. The media was now asking him: "Can you get it done? Do your teammates believe in you?" He was put on the defensive, as opposed to simply answering questions about the upcoming game. So there was a lot of pressure on him; and, I believe, he was putting added pressure on himself because he wanted to perform well.

Bubby Brister was on trial.

With Bubby, our practices didn't change much. They remained pretty loose. With guys like Shannon Sharpe on the team, things stayed loose and we were able to work and have fun at the same time. Humor is a welcome distraction for us. Our routine is the same, day in and day out, so a laugh here and there helps break the monotony. One of Shanahan's strong suits is that he changes up our offense so much from day to day and week to week that it keeps everything fresh. You're forced to pay close attention in order to get that extra advantage.

We made it through the next several games without any major problems. We continued to pile win after win onto our record. We remained undefeated. Bubby started four games and participated in three others, while John recovered from his hamstring injury and a back ailment. He stepped in and made a huge contribution to the team. The goal didn't change. We were 13-0 and shooting for another Super Bowl victory.

New York vs. Denver

Then we ran into a buzz saw in New York. That season, the Giants were a good, solid team, but they hadn't shown it in their previous games. They were better than their record reflected. Going into the game, we felt that we could beat them, but we didn't get it done. We didn't execute. Lack of execution in all phases of the game is the primary cause of most losses.

Everyone   was waiting for us to fall at

Lack of execution in all phases of the game is the primary cause of most losses.

that point. It was near the end of the regular season. The Giants knew they weren't going to the playoffs, and we knew we had a spot waiting for us. In fact, when teams played us, it was like a championship game for them— their "Super Bowl"—because it gave them an idea of how good their organization was, gave them something to compare themselves to. We would have loved to have gone undefeated, but I think fatigue set in.

We lost to the Giants 20-16.

Truthfully, there was some sense of relief after we lost. We no longer had that 10,000-pound monkey on our backs. I remember defensive tackle, Keith Traylor saying, "I'm happy that's off my back. It was wearing me down." And Neil Smith agreed: "It was a burden. And the burden was heavy." Now, the pressure was gone. We no longer had to answer those questions—how are you going to do it? Do you think you'll make it? It was crazy. We were able to get rid of all that exterior noise, move on, and start playing football again.

Denver vs. Miami

The following game against Miami, we dropped the ball again. We didn't have anything to play for. We had secured home-field advantage for the playoffs. We knew we had a shot at the Super Bowl. So we allowed Miami to take advantage. Basically, the Dolphins had played at a higher level. And although our playoff destiny was sealed, we needed to go out and play good football. We still needed to compete.

In the end, I think the two straight loses after a 13-0 start woke us up and got us back on track for the playoffs.

Denver vs. Seattle

Before the final game of the season against Seattle, Elway said: "It was crucial for us to get the winning feeling again and get over that hump of 13 wins." He was right. Somewhere along the way, we were approaching games as a chore. We were weighed down by all of the media attention. We beat Seattle 28-21 and got back on track. As a team, we regained our focus.

A week off also helped us to rest up and get ready for the playoffs.

Denver vs. Miami

We got our revenge on the Dolphins when they came to Mile High for the first playoff game. It was a big win for us. We had our fans behind us and were able to beat them in our own backyard, which was fine retribution for the earlier loss just weeks before. We wiped the slate clean with a final score of 38-3.

Next…we had to face the New York Jets.

AFC Championship Game
Denver vs. N.Y. Jets

In the AFC title game against the Jets, there was raw, visceral emotion in the stands. Everybody was hyped for this game. It was also Elway's game. Denver fans were hoping it wouldn't be John's last game at Mile High Stadium. There was a lot of speculation about his possible retirement. And from the Jets' perspective, they were ready to put an end to his career sooner rather than later.

Stats

Reprinted from *USA Today,* (January 15, 1999):

"**Game Plan:** *The Broncos made it their mission to 'win one for John' last year but might adopt the same attitude Sunday when Elway plays what probably is his final game at Mile High Stadium. It could be a big day for him as the Jets focus on slowing league MVP Terrell Davis. The Jets will try to make Elway beat them through the air. It could be a shootout, but the key will be Denver's cornerbacks, Darrien Gordon and Ray Crockett, and whether they can cover Keyshawn Johnson and Wayne Chrebet. If Curtis Martin has success early, it will open up play action for Vinny Testaverde and make things difficult for Denver's pass rush.*

"**Postseason record:** *N.Y. Jets improved to 6-6 after defeating Jacksonville 34-24 last week in the AFC divisional playoff game. Denver is 14-11.*

"**Series:** *Denver leads in the regular season 13-12-1; it's the teams' first postseason meeting. Denver won the last one 31-6 Sept. 1, 1996, at Mile High.*

"**Statistics:** *N.Y. Jets—Scored 416 points this season, second most in club history (419 in 1968). Martin rushed for 1,287 yards, second most in club history. The Jets have the AFC's top passing game (239.8). Denver—The Broncos have the No. 1 offense in the AFC and No. 3 overall. Denver averages 31.3 points a game to the Jets' 26.0."*

———————————

Leading up to this game, the New York Jets had a seven-game winning streak. They had scored an average of 29.6 points. I remember the night before the game, Shanahan said to us, "You guys know we can dominate any team we play…I'm so sick and tired of hearing what a great defense they have. Our defense will show what a great defense is."

Jets coach Bill Parcells prided himself on complex offensive schemes. When we study film of the Jets, we see everything. In

"Our defense will show what a great defense is."

their playoff win against the Jacksonville Jaguars, they

ran 77 plays from 38 formations. They had a new center, a new quarterback, and a new running back. They posed a threat to our Super Bowl dream.

In the first 30 minutes of the game, we were shut out completely. Then the game took a million twists and turns. The Jets committed six turnovers, a rookie had blocked Tom Rouen's punt at the Denver goal line with 12 minutes left in the third, and the Jets were ahead, 10-0. And the wind was going nuts at Mile High. Elway said it was the worst Denver wind he had ever experienced.

Things took a turn in our favor when Elway decided to do what he did best—he started slinging the ball. He was calm and methodical, and we all maintained our focus, which is difficult in high-stakes games. But we never panicked.

Shannon Sharpe was in the huddle getting everybody revved up. He screamed, "Here we go! This is for all the minicamps, for all the sprints we ran,

> *. . . we all maintained our focus, which is difficult in high-stakes games. But we never panicked.*

and all the weights we lifted! We're better than this!" Then when we went into the huddle for the first-down play from the Jets' 36-yard line, Ed McCaffrey and Rod Smith lined up opposite where they should have been. The two started to switch sides, but the play clock was running down, so Elway motioned to them, "Run each other's route." And they did.

Ed ended up being alone down the field when Elway threw a 47-yard completion. Two plays later, Elway threw a hard ball into my midsection, and I dove in for an 11-yard touchdown.

We were just getting warmed up.

Jason Elam had an incredible game that day, wind and all. At one point, he had intended to kick high, but the wind caught the ball, and it hit around the Jets' 20 and bounced back to the 30. Luckily, Keith Burns recovered it, and three plays later, Jason kicked a 44-yard field goal, which tied the score, 10-10.

We continued playing aggressively. Within a matter of minutes, we turned a 10-point deficit into a 10-point lead. We won the game, 23-10. We had reason to be proud. We had pulled through a game that was filled with challenges. Everybody stepped up in that game—Darrien Gordon, Jason Elam, Ed McCaffrey, Ray Crockett. Terrell

> *We had pulled through a game that was filled with challenges.*

finished with 167 yards on 32 carries.

After the game, Elway came over the PA system, screaming back to the fans, who had all gone berserk by then: "I love you!" The fans then started chanting, "Stay, John! Don't go!" It was such an emotional game all the way around. By the end of the night, John was all choked up. He hadn't formally announced whether he'd be back next season or not, but with all of the emotion that was in the stadium, it appeared that he had played his last game at Mile High.

Thinking back on the '98 season, it was quite remarkable. We had done things beyond our wildest imagination. It was evident that we had such a tight unit, that we were all—coaches and players—on the same page. After meeting all of the many challenges the season hurled our way, the Super Bowl didn't seem so daunting. We had pulled through tough situations all season long and had record-breaking success. Take Jason Elam in the Jacksonville game—he kicked the ball 63 yards into history. He had kicked that long in practice, but never in a game. All of us knew what Jason was capable of, but now the world knows. Take Bubby Brister and the accurate performances he pulled off in Elway's absence. We won every game he started.

Throughout the entire season, there was a serious accounting taking place of Terrell's yardage. When all was said and done, he ran for 2,008 yards, the third-highest single-season total in NFL history. He also topped the league in rushing TDs, total TDs, scoring, and first downs. The funny thing about Terrell is that he barely knows his numbers. But why should he? He has the entire sports community keeping tabs on him. I usually know his numbers better than he does. And my reasons for that are simple. His numbers are my numbers. They are a reflection of the job I've done blocking for him. I hang my hat on Terrell's numbers.

Headlines

"Griffith: 'Bodyguard' for Davis" Reprinted from *USA TODAY,* by Jarrett Bell (January 29, 1999):

"He is the football version of a Secret Service agent, the one lurking behind the scenes and keeping the main man away from danger. Rarely is he recognized, applauded or hailed by the masses. Yet it's a tough job, as they say, that somebody has to do. Meet Howard Griffith, the unsung hero of the Denver Broncos' offense, whose value as perhaps the NFL's best blocking back is a subtle complement to 2,000-yard rusher Terrell Davis....Griffith can be easily lost amid the high-profile stars on the AFC's highest-scoring offense. Davis is the reigning Super Bowl MVP and NFL MVP. John Elway is a household name under constant watch. Shannon Sharpe is a media magnet. Ed McCaffrey and Rod Smith make the highlight films, too.

"Says Griffith, 'People don't really notice what I do.' Davis notices. 'Wherever Howard is, I try to follow,' he says."

Super Bowl XXXIII

Miami, Florida

ATLANTA FALCONS VS. DENVER BRONCOS

Pro Player Stadium

JANUARY 31,1999

I was excited about the second Super Bowl journey. It was just as exciting as the first time, but in a different way.

We had nearly the same roster as we had for Super Bowl XXXII, which is so rare, considering free agency and salary cap issues. We were missing only three starters—Brian Habib and Allen Aldridge, who had gone on to other teams, and Gary Zimmerman, who had retired.

In any championship game, you have the feeling that you're going out there with the chance of being a hero or…. a goat. So the adrenaline rush, the nerves, and the worries are always there. However, we felt strongly that we could win this game. We believed that we were the better team, and all we needed to do was go out and execute our game plan. We studied and practiced the game plan for two weeks. In fact, we were tired of running it. But we continued to go over and over the plays. So, by the time we arrived in Miami we were totally prepared.

Thinking back, going through the whole season, moving up the ranks, dealing with the pressure and high expectations of being the championship team, the second time around was more of a chore than the exciting, thrilling ride of the first championship victory. It was more work. And in many ways, it is a lot tougher trying to win your second championship than your first. The fun factor is not there. Everyone is looking to beat you. You're a target for hungry young teams vying for that trophy.

Nonetheless, once a champion, always a champion. You want to continue to win as long as you can. You just have to consider different motivators—solid reasons to continue to work hard and fight hard to hold on to your championship status.

The media hype during this championship was all about Mike Shanahan and the Falcons' coach, Dan Reeves; Elway and Reeves; Terrell Davis

> *In many ways, it is a lot tougher trying to win your second championship than your first.*

and Jamal Anderson. It was a completely different scene from our first Super Bowl experience, because many of the stories that were making the news had so little to do with football. There were all of these personal stories about the opening of old wounds, settling personal vendettas, rivalry and pride. It was a highly unusual scene.

I remember watching television one day, and someone said he'd rather see Denver and Atlanta in the Super Bowl than Denver and Minnesota. And the thought immediately occurred to me that the only reason they want to see that is to keep all of the stories swirling about Elway, Reeves, and Shanahan. That matchup would make all of the sportswriters' jobs quite easy. The stories would write themselves. Playing against Minnesota would have been all X's and O's. It wouldn't have had the same dramatic subplot.

By game day, everything that could have been said was said, all kinds of negative words exchanged and personal feelings made public. Some would say that all of the events leading up to the game made for a more interesting competition. But the fact remained, we still had a game to play.

The foundation of the Falcons' game plan appeared to be "Stop Terrell Davis." They assumed that in our biggest game of the year, to score points, we'd give the ball to Terrell. But we were more creative than that. It all gets back to matchups. People continue to underestimate the ability of players like Rod Smith and Ed McCaffrey. I think we force teams to bring more to the table. The fact of the matter was that we had Rod Smith, Ed McCaffrey, Shannon Sharpe, *and* Terrell Davis. Then, we could always bring in Willie Green. The intention was to go in, run the game plan, execute it, and score.

We did the job we came to do.

Part of our game plan was to utilize me more, since we knew they'd be going after Terrell. Shanahan used me in several new formations. With Terrell attracting so much of the Falcons' attention, I was able to score on our first possession from the 1-yard line. In the fourth quarter, we ran the same play, and I scored a second time, giving us a 24-6 lead.

Terrell and I have developed

> *The intention is to go in, run the game plan, execute it, and score.*

such great communication over the past few years. After working so closely together, by the time the Super Bowl rolled around, we were able to communicate nonverbally, on instinct. I remember one play in which I noticed how the guys were lined up, so I said, "Terrell, this guy is up on the line of scrimmage. I'm going to have to cut him." For me, the best approach is to cut that guy because if I take him on high, even if I win, he's three yards deep in the backfield. So Terrell needs to get a clean look. The best way for him to get a clean look is for me to cover him. We talk about every aspect of our game. We examine every possible scenario. I'll say to him:

"You need to set them up because I'm going to go for his outside shoulder to force him wide, and you keep running like you're going real wide, then come underneath."

One of the things Terrell and I both try to do is anticipate what defenses are going to try to do to us. Because we know if I line up in a certain formation and they think a particular play is coming, they get the edge. That means I need to adjust my stance to make it look like it's a run. But maybe it's a pass. That makes it more challenging for your opponent.

The working relationship that Terrell and I have developed over the years is evident in our productivity. When you consider the outside influences that affect national sports in general— media hype, outrageous salaries and the public disclosure of those salaries, product endorsements, corporate sponsorships, and all that, it's easy to forget yourself. They can be huge distractions. But Terrell and I have great respect for each other. We have not encountered the difficulties that are often part of playing with a high-profile player. No matter what's going on in a game, he has always respected me as a player. He is smart enough to realize that you cannot alienate other players. There are times, of course, when I don't do as good a job as I'd like, and it affects his results. Then again, there are times that I play at the top of my game, doing the best job I know how, and he can't perform the way he'd like. So it's a game of give-and-take.

I have always believed in approaching any difference of opinion with a measure of respect. You have to maintain the attitude of a team player and consider at all times what is best for the team. If there is inner conflict, it's bound to have a trickle-down effect, which could eventually adversely affect productivity.

Back to Atlanta. Although we lost Shannon Sharpe to a knee injury, we were able to continue our run and finally walk away, once more, as the Super Bowl champs.

I think John Mobley said it best: "The Dirty Bird's dead. We plucked them turkeys."

It was a great win for us. It solidified our place in NFL history and proved to the world that the Denver Broncos were the best team in the league.

> *I have always believed in approaching any difference of opinion with a measure of respect.*

We had fought hard in the championship game against Green Bay and had showed the world just what we were made of, but against Atlanta we were the champions going in. It's an entirely different issue *defending* a title rather than *winning* one.

DENVER	7	10	0	17	34
Atlanta	3	3	0	13	19

It's great when you're winning. Cameras are flashing all over the place, everybody wants to hear what you have to say. The media are swarming all around you: "Hey, we want you to do our show." The one question I was asked the most that night was: "Why aren't you talking more about yourself?" They couldn't understand it. I was talking about the game, the plays, and the team, all of which is good press for the coach. But they felt this was my day in the sun, so they wanted to hear, "Hey, it's me, Howard Griffith. Did you catch my two touchdown plays?" But that's not where my head was.

It didn't hit me until the next day.

Reporters who are unfamiliar with your NFL background usually take more time talking to you than reporters who know your history. The rain saved me that night. I had gone out on the field and completed two interviews, but when it started raining, I cut out to the locker room.

But I was still one of the last guys to get back to the hotel because of the all the interview requests. And although I did a ton of them, in the locker room, there were still a lot of interviews I bypassed because I was ready to get out of there and be with my family.

It's funny, I don't remember being as emotional the second time around. The setup was different in Miami. Our hotels were in Ft. Lauderdale, so just getting back there in all the traffic was difficult.

The feeling after the game was similar to a win at home. Usually, after a home game, unless we have out-of-town guests, I go back to the house and go to sleep. The ride home from the game was so long, I almost fell asleep.

I was glad it was over.

There's so much buildup each year at Super Bowl time that when it's over, you are thoroughly exhausted. I could even see the relief in Shanahan's face. He was too smart to actually say it, but we knew beforehand that unless things deteriorated completely, we could beat Atlanta.

But that's not to say that we took the Falcons for granted. In big games, anything can happen. There is often a minute's difference between winning and losing, winning by the skin of your teeth, and completely dominating a team. The difference can be a single play or that extra preparation you put in.

SIDELINE

Mike Bellamy,
Former Illinois Wide Receiver/
Former Philadelphia Eagle

"I was determined to go to the Super Bowl in Miami. It was really important that I be there. I told my wife, 'I don't care what I have to do to get tickets.' I ended up on the 50-yard line, five rows behind the bench. And I think I must have taken about 25 pictures of Howard right on the sideline, just because of my excitement. Seeing somebody achieve the dream we've all wanted to achieve. It was incredible.

"Then I remembered looking in *USA Today* in the week leading up to the game, and they named all of the backs Howard had blocked for. All of them had 1,000-yard and 2,000-yard seasons. And of course, the running backs are going to get all of the press clippings. But Howard helped all of those players get what they got. He is the epitome of a team player."

Between the two championship victories, the second Super Bowl win will always stand out in my mind. I was able to get the ball and actually contribute, in a big way, to that game's final result. I had the chance to score a couple of touchdowns in the game, which will be my mark in the history books, that short moment documented on film that will be shown over and over for years to come. That's a fantastic personal victory.

SIDELINE

Karen Chilton,
Howard's sister-in-law

"Sitting in the stands after Howard's first touchdown, we were all going crazy. But when he scored the second time, I remember turning to his father and saying: 'Did you think Howard was going to score *two* touchdowns in this game?' And his reply: 'No. I only told him to get one!' We were so happy for him. In fact, our whole section became Howard Griffith fans by the time it was over. Fans were asking to take pictures with his jersey, which I had carried with me to the game. That jersey got passed around so many times...and I actually got offers from people to buy it. Only at the Super Bowl."

SIDELINE

Dr. J. W. Smith,
Former Head Football Coach,
Percy L. Julian High School

"When Howard got on that field in Super Bowl XXXII in San Diego, I was so proud. I was just swelling. I swear, I took up two seats. But my proudest moment was when Howard scored two touchdowns in the second Super Bowl. He'd prepared for any eventuality. So when he had to carry the ball, he did it. When he had to catch passes out of the backfield, he did that. But mainly, he was a blocking back. And now, he's one of the best in the league."

SIDELINE

Shannon Sharpe,
Tight End, Baltimore Ravens

"Griff has been an unsung hero on this team for so long, it was great to see him get the touchdowns."

SIDELINE

Bucky Godbolt,
Former Illinois Running Back Coach

"He learned a long time ago. There was probably somebody along the way who got in his head when they said, 'You are not going to make it. You are not good enough. You are going to go to a school and get Prop 48. You are going to sit out. You are never going to make it. You are never going to graduate.' Those things weighed heavy in his mind. And he said, 'OK, you say that I can't? I'm going to show you that I can.' And that is what he has done. I'm sure there are people even today at the University of Illinois who say, 'I can't believe this guy has made it this long. How the heck does he do it?'

"Carolina said: 'He's just a journeyman. We got enough out of him. Time to move him out.' Well, let me tell you how journeyed he is. He is now probably in the top two or three fullbacks of football right now."

Headlines

"Super Bowl XXXIII- Ron Meyer's Analysis", reprinted from

CNN Sports Illustrated webpage (CNNSI.com):

"I walked into a press conference of Dan Reeves Wednesday morn-ing and he was talking about this back who was really a professional who did everything—could block, could catch the ball, could run with authority. I started taking notes on Terrell Davis and it was Howard Griffith he was talking about. This guy is really, in Dan Reeves' mind, when he was talking about him, one of the best ever. And he certainly proved that point today."

The issue of "getting credit" continued to come up for me after the Super Bowl. In fact, it is the one question I am always asked: "How do you handle standing in the shadows? Being the unsung hero?"

Well, it's just one of those things. I know my position and I'm comfortable in my position. It's not a marquee position. After scoring two TDs in the Super Bowl, I didn't even have a photo in *Sports Illustrated.* So, I didn't bother to read the article. If you look in a sports magazine, there may be stories about the Broncos, and maybe a sentence or two about me, or perhaps a small snapshot...if I'm lucky. But I realized a long time ago that so many factors go into becoming the "celebrity" athlete, many of which have abso-lutely nothing to do with your record or performance. You can work hard to get to that next level, but the media and those in control must be willing to see you there.

We're living in an interesting time where people, fans, audiences don't necessarily decide what they like or don't like. They're bombarded by images on television, in film, on the Internet, and basically are told what to like, what to buy, what to support. So becoming a media star is a career all in itself. Usually, the media will mention John Elway and the receivers. But when you talk about the running game, you talk about the tailback and the offensive line. So, the fullback always

I realized a long time ago that so many factors go into becoming the "celebrity" athlete . . .

gets lost in the equation, except perhaps in Dallas with "Moose." Daryl Johnston did a lot to bring attention to the importance of the position. Because of his reputation, whenever he touched the ball, everybody screamed.

On the local level, I am well received by Broncos fans. When I'm going in or coming out of the stadium, doing autograph signings and personal appearances, the fans come out. And they're the first to say: "You don't get enough credit. You're the reason this happened or that happened." And they know. It's frustrating at times, but you get used to it. One thing I can say about the Denver Broncos, is the guys on the team who get the national attention deserve it. Take Shannon Sharpe, when he's done playing, he will be considered the best tight end ever to play the game.

Headlines

"Broncos Display Super Consistency," reprinted from *USA Today,* by Jarrett Bell, February 2, 1999:

"The Broncos surely deserve a sigh of relief after becoming the seventh Super Bowl champion to successfully defend its crown. And while they head toward next season, pondering the possibility of becoming the first team to produce a "three-peat" Super Bowl run, the Broncos already have assured themselves a special place in history."

Three-Year Plan

With their Super Bowl XXXIII crown, the Denver Broncos set an NFL record for most victories over a three-year span (46), including the postseason. The best "three-year" teams:

Team (Years)	Victories
Denver Broncos (1996-98)	*46*
S.F. 49ers (1988-1990)	*45*

Miami Dolphins (1971-73)	*44*
Dallas Cowboys (1992-1994)	*44*

(Source: *USA Today* Research)

It was a long season. By the time you get to December, you're sore and hurting, so when the playoffs roll around, you're just happy that you're still able to play. When it's all over, you look forward to the time off.

GRIFF NOTES

The Win

When you get that call. When you've sold that product or idea, graduated from college, or won a championship. Whatever the goal is that you set out to accomplish, you win once you've successfully executed your game plan. Your dream has been fulfilled. From the game plan, from putting your roster together, going over your drills, preparing before the game, and going out on the field to get that first down—score after score, goal after goal, when the final score is in and you're on top, you've won.

There is this idea that you have to win at all costs, succeed at any price—I believe that winning requires that you do things the right way. It's like the old adage: Hard work pays off. In my journey, I've never seen a quick fix or any tricks of the trade that can bring about an easy win. Winning takes hard work and dedication, a well-conceived game plan, and a well-planned series of actions to execute that plan. I remember when I was in high school, there were a few players who thought by taking steroids, they'd enhance their performance. Well, they were already playing backup positions, and the steroids cost them their careers. They were both released from the squad.

There's nothing like setting out to achieve a goal, putting in the time and effort to make it happen, then seeing that goal actualized.

G = Getting

O = Over

A = All

L = Limitations

- Hard work is a given.

- Patience is often a difficult proposition, but necessary and unavoidable.

- There are no true limitations, other than the ones you place on yourself.

- Motivation and dedication can't be bought. You have to acquire them on your own by participating in activities that keep you focused and by incorporating positive philosophies that inspire and uplift.

Remember:

It takes guts to stick it out in the face of opposition and seemingly impenetrable barriers, but it makes the success all the sweeter. The real work is to keep your goal in sight at all times, and keep it moving.

Be about the business of taking an active role in the realization of your goal. Bring something to table, your special skills and talents that will add to the total team equation. Expect to be challenged by obstacles and unexpected challenges, but prepare in advance so you can tackle each and every barrier effectively and efficiently.

Winning is a formidable task. It doesn't come easy. It takes hard work and perseverance. But the good news is: Focus, dedication, and a real commitment to the set goal guarantees success.

FINAL NOTES

ELWAY. WILL HE OR WON'T HE RETURN?

My initial impression was that John would come back because there was so much pressure on him to break the NFL record, by winning three consecutive Super Bowls. That prospect alone made it very tempting, I'm sure. There was also the addition of Dale Carter to the team, who everyone expected to make a huge difference on defense.

My dad was already talking about Atlanta. "Well, the Super Bowl's in Atlanta this year, gotta get some tickets," he said.

I knew better.

I told him, "We better wait and see how things pan out."

Needless to say, things turned out differently.

In fact, the Broncos' entire house of cards began to crumble.

Broncos Schedule 1999-2000

Week 1	**Miami**
Week 2	**At Kansas City**
Week 3	**At Tampa Bay**
Week 4	**NY Jets**
Week 5	**At Oakland**
Week 6	**Green Bay**
Week 7	**At New England**
Week 8	**Minnesota**
Week 9	**At San Diego**
Week 10	**At Seattle**
Week 11	**Cincinnati**
Week 12	**Kansas City**
Week 13	**At Jacksonville**
Week 14	**Seattle**
Week 15	**At Detroit**
Week 16	**San Diego**

When Elway decided to step down, the team dynamic changed almost immediately. The next big shock to our system came when Steve Atwater was released. If you ask anyone on the team, they'll tell you that Atwater was right behind Elway when it came to Denver football. If Elway was the No. 1 favorite, Atwater was No. 2, as far as the fans were concerned.

Players began to feel that if it could happen to Atwater, it could happen to anybody. Again, football is a business. It's not always about personal feelings, friendships, loyalties, or alliances. It is, and always will be, about the bottom line—the almighty dollar. Steve handled it well. He took the high road. He could have gone ballistic, and we would have all backed him up. I don't think any of us wanted to see him leave. He handled it the best way he knew how, but you could look at him and tell that he was burned up about it. He had been with Denver his entire professional career. He gave the organization a lot of years. And for his team, he was a leader.

So, there we were, minus two team leaders—our offensive and defensive captains.

The final blow came with the release of our special-teams captain, Keith Burns. By this time, the consensus among the players was that the season would be a struggle. We had lost three central players, and our roster just wasn't as tight as it had been. Our success in the previous two seasons was predicated on consistency. You don't necessarily have to have the fastest guy on the team, but you do have to have the player who understands his role and the team's game plan.

> **By this time, the consensus among the players was that the season would be a struggle.**

The whole organization seemed to be in transition. Change had set in.

We also lost our starting right tackle, Harry Swayne. So many players were missing who had been pivotal in our success. We figured there was no way we'd have the same kind of season in '99 that we had experienced in the previous two years.

I predicted early on that it was not going to be the season that everyone wanted it to be.

I knew we were in trouble in the preseason. In fact, when we played in Australia, I knew trouble was waiting right around the corner. We just weren't the same team. You can't underestimate the importance of camaraderie. You may be able to get players to play positions, but even talent isn't a substitute for chemistry. When you disrupt the chemistry—the elements that make up a team dynamic—you can't rely on the outcome.

We were doomed from the beginning of the season.

First of all, replacing John Elway puts you in a no-win situation.

We lost a Hall of Fame-caliber quarterback, along with two other team leaders, yet we were still expected to go out and win a championship. It wasn't going to happen.

Adding fuel to the fire was the whole Brian Griese/Bubby Brister quarterback debate. Originally, the entire team believed that Bubby would take over for John Elway. It was a natural next step for Bubby because he had played so well in games where he had to step in for John; his record was solid. He was the top quarterback

You can't underestimate the importance of camaraderie.

in camp, as well as at the beginning of the preseason. Then, toward the end of the preseason, he was benched for Brian Griese.

I still believe it wasn't the fact that the switch happened; rather it was the way it happened that caused dissension throughout the organization.

We all knew going into the first game of the season that Brian had strong skills, that he had all the makings of an outstanding NFL quarterback. But those of us who had been around the game for a while knew that it was going to be extremely tough for him because everyone was gunning for us. We were the two-time Super Bowl champions. We were the team everyone wanted to pull down off the throne. And we had a tough season schedule ahead.

Hindsight is 20/20. In retrospect, we could see where many of our mistakes were, but who really knows? We may have ended up with the same record if Bubby had led the team. We'll never know. But from a team standpoint, it probably would have been better all the way around if Bubby and Brian could have had the opportunity to compete against each other for the starting job in camp and in the preseason. It may have been better for the whole team. But Bubby was benched without the team's knowledge, without a discussion or explanation, and that's what infuriated a lot of players. It sent the wrong message to the entire team.

> *We were the team everyone wanted to pull down off the throne.*

In my opinion, it was also unfair to Brian Griese. He was put on the hot seat and was nearly stifled by extremely high expectations from the team, the media, and the fans. He was criticized at every turn. He was in the unenviable position of being challenged constantly, being compared to his Hall of Fame father, Bob Griese, and the much-loved and well-respected Hall of Fame-caliber quarterback, John Elway.

After every game, all of the Monday-morning quarterbacks would say he should have done this or that, or his choices were bad, his rhythm was off. He was expected to be a winner and a savior, even though all the cards were stacked against him.

It was a difficult situation for us all.

It didn't help matters that we suffered multiple team injuries. Out for the season: Terrell Davis, John Mobley, Alfred Williams, and Shannon Sharpe. You couple that with a new quarterback, and you lose your winning combination.

There were times when I'd come to the offensive huddle, look around, and there'd be all new faces. I remember once, none of the guys who had been to the Super Bowl were in the huddle. Shannon was gone, Terrell, Rod may have missed a game, Ed McCaffrey missed one, Tony Jones was out for a few games—guys were dropping like flies. There were times we'd be in an intense game, trying to come from behind in the fourth quarter, and we'd have receivers on the field who were young, inexperienced players. It was tough for them because they were thrown into situations they had never experienced. There were several young guys on the team who stepped up, including Dwayne Carswell, Byron Chamberlain and Al Wilson. Olandis Gary managed to do an outstanding job despite the fact that the team was falling down around him. The up side is that they're ready now. They were able to learn, and they'll be better players in the future because of what they endured early on.

Despite it all, there was one event during the season that will always stand out in my mind as the highlight—the birth of my second son, Houston. Days before he was born, I had made it clear to the coaching staff that I planned to be with my wife for the birth, game or no game. Some debate began to stir about my decision in the Broncos organization and among the sports media. The *Denver Post* ran an article with a headline that read: "Griffith will be expecting call of a lifetime."

Coach Shanahan understood where I was coming from. He commented to the press, "First of all, I have the utmost respect for Howard. The way he practices, the way he handles himself. I respect Howard's decision . . . I have very strong feelings, but I think it's a product of how you were raised and what your beliefs are. I respect people's opinions when it comes to that area; there is not a right or wrong answer there. You just have to do what you feel is right."

I had missed the birth of little Howard; he was born in Chicago while I was at a Panthers away game in San Francisco. It still bothers me that I wasn't there. So I was determined that this time would be different. Naturally, I was hoping that there wouldn't be a conflict, though there was a slight possibility that Houston would come into the world smack dab in the middle of the Kansas City game.

Kim was due that week, and we were were both praying that I wouldn't be out on the field when it happened. As a precaution, I asked the team chaplain, Bill Rader, to hold my pager on the sidelines during the game. I didn't want to have to make the decision, but my mind was made up. If the pager went off, I was walking out of Mile High Stadium and heading straight to Rose Medical Center.

Fortunately, Houston entered the scene two days after the game on December 7, 1999. I took one look at him in the hospital and at my other son, Howard II, and everything was once again in its proper perspective. Needless to say, football was the last thing on my mind.

After our '99 season, Mike Shanahan came under a lot of criticism as well. The consensus was that he should have brought in a veteran quarterback. He tried to address some of those issues during one of our last meetings of the season. He didn't admit to making "wrong" decisions, but felt he had handled the decisions badly. I think he recognized, in retrospect, the importance of communicating with his players, and letting them know what your feelings are. It was something he failed to do in our abysmal '99 season.

Shanahan also had salary-cap issues to deal with, which accounts for certain players being cut and others coming on board.

I think he realized the importance of communicating with his players.

In my opinion, if I were the guy in charge, I'd approach the entire situation selfishly. I'd want the same guys who had won the Super Bowl championships with me. I'd want them all back. And I'd do all I could in order to keep them. Obviously, you want to get better year after year, but you need your core people, your players who understand their roles. You need them. And you have to find a way to keep them. It's hard to find players who are huge locker-room motivators, huge difference-makers on the field, and team leaders—you just don't find true leaders every day. Once you've got them, you have to do whatever you can to keep them on your squad.

It was especially difficult for Broncos fans because the Broncos have not been, in recent years, a losing team. The Broncos haven't been in a deficit situation, losing games the way we were losing them in the '99 season. It was frustrating every way you looked at it. And the finger pointing never ended. When it was all said and done, we were all blamed, one way or another, for a lousy season.

Up until this point, the Broncos have built this team by locking guys in for the long haul. But when players begin to feel that they should make a lot more money, sooner or later, they're going to stop signing long-term contracts. Everybody talks about how great

the organization is, and it's true— it is a good organization. But the fact remains,

When it was all said and done, we were all blamed, one way or another, for a lousy season.

when you have great players who are coming up on the last year of their contracts, things will change. Just think if Rod Smith didn't sign his extension. He could go out and demand $5 million a year and get it from a team that could use a player of his caliber. But instead, he chose to stay in Denver because he's happy in Denver. It's not always going to be that easy.

When you have your best players playing, obviously, your opportunities are going to be greater. But I think for the stretch of time that Bubby played, he proved that he could get it done. But now, it's a totally different game. Defenses are going to prepare differently. No one is going to allow you to continue to win championships without putting up a big fight. No one is going to allow Terrell to continue running, season after season, for 1,000 yards without challenging him.

The final accounting of the '99 season:

Won   6   Lost   10

Football is competitive.

You must have a game plan that incorporates not just one idea, but several. And you've got to have a backup plan. You've got to be creative to maintain your edge.

With the years comes experience. After awhile, your instincts are just so sharp. You've been in certain situations before, so you know how to gauge them. Some just do it quicker. The average person may see 50 pictures, while a Walter Payton might have seen 300 pictures in front of him. He'd have broken it down into so many different categories and so many angles that he'd have been able to see it all and make his move before anyone else.

SIDELINE

Randall Townsel,
Friend/Former Julian Football Player

"Howard is a professional. He's going to do his job—whether that means to make the block that frees up an all-pro tailback, or to make a one-handed, left-hand catch and not make a big deal of it even though it led to an AFC championship win, or whether it's to score two touchdowns in a Super Bowl and not make that a big deal, either. Howard's going to get the job done. And my favorite team is whatever teams he's on."

SIDELINE

David Paoni
Friend/Illinois graduate

"Howard is a student of the game and fit in well with every team he played for and thus was a silent leader who led by his example and his work ethic. When Howard finally made it to the top of his position, he treated each day like 'going to the office.' I remember phone calls early from Howard when he was not happy being overlooked by everyone and not playing. Howard would say to me that he was good, and it would one day show as long as he stayed focused.

"Howard does everything professionally and above board, which means that he can be a team player and an individual star at the same time. In the business world, characteristics like that make leaders and millionaires out of people. And I have no doubt that when Howard ends his great career, he will have another one waiting for him, no matter what he does. Howard can be anything he wants to be: coach, analyst, business man, financier, etc. You don't find people like that everyday. "

SIDELINE

Henry Jones,
Defensive Back, Buffalo Bills

"The biggest pressure playing in the NFL is to perform. We're under a microscope and everybody's watching—the owner, the coaches, the general manager, your peers in the league, your teammates, your family, and you. As players we tend to put most of the pressure on ourselves. I want to be the best safety in the league, and when I feel like I'm not doing my best, on comes the pressure.

"Howard and I share a bond because we come from similar places, the city of Chicago, the city of St. Louis, to the U of I. We spent countless hours together: eating, practicing, going to class, partying, or just chillin' in the yard. We overcame obstacles, school immaturity, coaching changes, and all of the pitfalls involved in major college athletics. We shared blood, sweat, and tears on the football field to make it to the NFL and to stay in it as long as we have."

SIDELINE

Huie Griffith,
Howard's father

"When it's all said and done, the number-one game on my list of great memories is not necessarily either of the Super Bowls. The number-one game was the one against Simeon High School. Five overtimes! Taylor Bell, the *Chicago Sun-Times* sportswriter, was sitting next to me. And I said to him: *"That's my son."*

Football is 5 percent physical and 95 percent mental. In my opinion, it is the greatest sport ever created. It demands that all 11 players do their assigned job at the same time, all the time, in order to achieve success. It is the ultimate team sport. Each player must be able to decipher the opponent's next move, then respond appropriately. If one player fails at his job, the other players must step up to strengthen the weak link.

It takes an entire team to win. And it takes a team player to contribute to that victory.

Everyone plays a part.

Career Chronology

(reprinted from the Denver Broncos website: DenverBroncos.com)

HOWARD GRIFFITH

1999-2000

DENVER BRONCOS—FULLBACK

Among the most significant acquisitions made by Broncos head coach Mike Shanahan in '97 was that of fullback Howard Griffith, who lived up to his reputation as the best blocking fullback in pro football.

1998-1999

DENVER BRONCOS—FULLBACK

Griffith started at fullback in 13 of 16 games and played in 14, rushing four times for 13 yards (3.3.), with a long of 16 (the longest rush of his career at NYG) while catching 15 passes for 97 yards (6.5) including a long of 15 (vs. N.E.) and three touchdowns. Griffith's primary contributions came as a blocking back in support of the Broncos' overall running game, which ranked second in the NFL with an average of 154.3 yards per game. Postseason: Griffith started at fullback in both postseason games and caught two passes for 25 yards while providing stellar lead blocking for a dominant rushing attack that has averaged 214 yards per game as a team through two playoff contests. He caught one pass for 14 yards while paving the way for Terrell Davis in his franchise postseason-record 199-yard rushing performance in the AFC Divisional Playoff Game vs. Miami, and caught another for 11 yards in the AFC Championship Game vs. the Jets.

1997-1998
DENVER BRONCOS—FULLBACK

Griffith played in 15 of 16 games and made 13 starts at fullback in his first year in Denver, opening holes for Terrell Davis while shouldering his share of the offensive load. For the year, he rushed nine times for 34 yards (3.8), with a long of nine yards (vs. K.S.), and caught 11 passes for 55 yards (5.0) with a long of 20 (vs. Oakland). He paved the way for a franchise-record 10 100-yard rushing games by backfield mate Terrell Davis, including two 200-yard efforts (vs. Cinc. and at Buff.).

1996-1997

Griffith started 14 of 16 games for Carolina, with his only two non-starts coming in games where the Panthers opened in a three-receiver formation. For the season, he rushed 12 times for seven yards with one touchdown. He set career highs for both receptions (27) and receiving yards (223), and scored one receiving touchdown. Perhaps his greatest contribution was the devastating blocking he provided for tailback Anthony Johnson, who logged 1,120 yards for the year.

1995-1996
CAROLINA PANTHERS—FULLBACK

Griffith was selected in the 1995 expansion draft. He set career highs in rushing yards and attempts with 197 yards on 65 carries while highlighting his ability as a blocker and serving as an important part of the Panthers offense.

1994-1995
L.A. RAMS

Griffith started 10 games as a fullback for the Rams, where he helped clear the way for All-Pro Jerome Bettis, who rushed for more than 1,000 yards for the second consecutive season. Griffith caught 16 passes, including his first career touchdown in a game vs. the Denver Broncos, a three-yard pass from Chris Chandler that gave the Rams a 27-21 victory. His nine rushes for 30 yards were the first of his career.

1993-1994

L.A. RAMS

Griffith signed as a free agent with the Rams, where he played special teams, returning eight kickoffs for 169 yards (21.1—second best on the squad.

1992-1993

SAN DIEGO CHARGERS

Griffith signed on the Chargers practice squad where he remained for the rest of the season.

1991

BUFFALO BILLS

Drafted by the Indianapolis Colts in the ninth round, Griffith was waived in training camp and was signed to the Bills' practice squad where he was a part of Buffalo's 1991 AFC Championship.

1991

INDIANAPOLIS COLTS

COLLEGE

UNIVERSITY OF ILLINOIS

Griffith finished his career at Illinois with school records for career touchdowns (33), touchdowns in a season (15), and single-game rushing yards (26.3). During his senior season (1990) Griffith set an NCAA record with eight touchdowns vs. Southern Illinois. As a junior (1989) he ranked second on the team with 39 catches for 287 yards and earned the *Sporting News* All-American Honorable Mention.

HIGH SCHOOL

PERCY L. JULIAN HIGH SCHOOL

An all-conference running back at Percy Julian High School in Chicago. Griffith also lettered three years in baseball.

AWARDS

1998   NFL "UNSUNG HERO" Award Recipient